Bowmanville's Octagon House

From Church, Faith & Tait
to
Irwin & Seto

JANICE SETO

The Atelier
Bowmanville, Ontario, Canada

Copyright © 2016 Janice Seto

Bowmanville's Octagon House: From Church, Faith & Tait to Irwin & Seto

ISBN-13: 978-1926935195 (book)
ISBN-13: 978-1-926935-20-1 (ebook)

License Notes

Disclaimer

Dedication

Dad
(Johnny Seto, 'King of the Coronation')

And

The Irwin Family
(for the keys to the castle)

Preface by Janice Seto

Octagon houses require so much elbow grease. More than likely, an octagon house has historic designation, including this one in Bowmanville. For some people, such as designation is a benefit; for others, it is a bane. Unless your residence is so designated, you have no idea the restrictions and obligations that come with the label 'historical'. Elements that seem superfluous to the amateur eye (the owner's) when it comes to renovations turn out to be of great interest to municipal authorities.

Truth be told, everyone has an opinion on ths unique historical home. It may be your place but it seems everyone else has a say in it.

 And they express them - from innocuous dogwalkers to the local paper to tourists driving by who do a double-take - "What is this place?" – and then park their car and ring the doorbell, curious about this private residence.

Then there is maintenance. It always takes more time when calling for a quotation for, let's say, roofing: "It is not a joke - it is an eight-sided roof for an eight-sided house."

"I never been inside an octagon house… Tell me about it…"

In this book, I share with you images of what I have learnt so far about Bowmanville's Octagon House… Something about its uniqueness has over 150 years attracted creative, community-oriented people. Here was nurtured the young Alice Freeman who became Canada's first female columnist as Faith Fenton, one of the most influential journalists in her day. Henry Tait, photographer. Musical salons and prayer meetings. Young couples getting their start. Gardeners. Grandmothers. Now in its 2nd century, let us peer inside Bowmanville's Octagon House…

Contents

ACKNOWLEDGEMENTS

Ellen Puerzer, author of The Octagon House Inventory, and Robert Kline webmaster of The Octagon House Inventory website

David Webber

Grant Trolley & Ron Chow, Facebook group: Bowmanville in the 60s and 70s

Judy (Vinish) Mann

Charles Taws

Michael McAdam & The Clarington Museums & Archives

My family

Michael Kellawan, all the best

Many images in this book are unfortunately fuzzy due to a great variety of sources

Chapter 1: Health has 8 Sides: Octagonal Houses

Hexagonal (stop sign-shape) and octagonal-shaped structures through the ages in many different cultures usually serve cultural or religious purposes. Constructing a circular structure in historical times was not something lightly attempted – corners being avoided in a circle and it is said that the devil hides in corners, so an eight-sided building was an acceptable substitute.

An example of this is found in Italy, the Lateran Baptistery (San Giovanni in Fonte, Rome) built circa 432 by pop Sixtus II[i]. Another octagonal building that is more widely seen on news broadcasts is the shrine known as the Dome of the Rock (Qubbat As-Sakrah) overlooking Jerusalem.

Other octagonal structures are outside gazebos and even storehouses, an example being the 'Little Round House' on the campus of the University of Alabama.

It was only in the mid-1850s that octagonal building as the ideal family residence came into vogue – for health reasons. This was the idea of Orson Squires Fowler (1809-1887), who hailed from the western New York State area known as the Burned Over District. According to historian John T Martin[ii], this was frontier land in theearly 1800s around the time of the building of the Erie Canal, settled by English-speaking Protestants with few priested Episcopalian clergy. Lacking spiritual direction, these people was on their own, leading to various layperson-led revivals and converts to Congregationalists, Baptists, and Methodist. Evangelism was so prevalent to that Charles Grandison Finney thought there was no one left to 'burn' (convert), and thus the district was 'burned out'. During this time emerged new religious callings such as Joseph Smith (Mormon), William Miller (Seventh-Day Adventists and Jehovah's Witness), séances.

OCTAGON HOUSE C.1905

Located at 48 Division Street, this house represents an architectural style that is rare in Ontario. The eight-sided octagon design was promoted by an eccentric American, named Orson Squire Fowler, in the 1850s. Essentially, Mr. Fowler felt that a traditional house, where items piled up unhandily in the corners, caused bad temperament among the occupants. They, in turn, soured the temperament of their children *"Thus rendering the whole family bad dispositioned by nature"* as he lamented in his book about the virtues of octagon buildings.

Mr. Fowler's concepts were never enthusiastically taken up by the masses, but a small number of octagonal houses, barns, and even outhouses, were built in Ontario.

Figure 1. Charles Taws, Bowmanville Then and Now, 1998

Franz Joseph Gall, a Vienna physician, invented what later was known as phrenology ('science of the mind'): character was based on brain shape – and postulated that skull shape somehow responded to brain shape. The notoriety of being banned from teaching this in 1802 made Gall's ideas even more popular. American James Biddle brought phrenology to the States in 1806. By examining someone's skull, the new science of phrenology, according to Johann Gaspar Spurzheim, a pupil of Gall, one can discern someone's character, and possibly influence it. Fowler wrote his own book on phrenology in 1836 based on translations of Gall and Spurzheim and published *American Phrenological Journal and Miscellany* (ceased only in 1911).

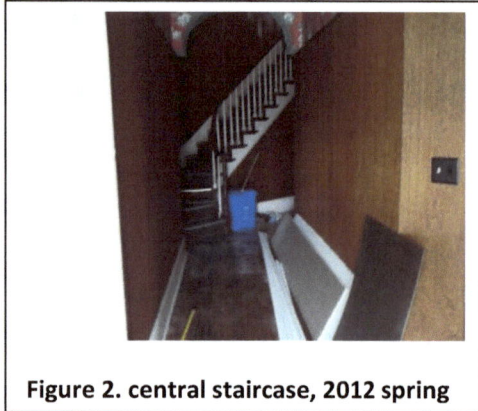

Figure 2. central staircase, 2012 spring

Fowler, whose writings fed his popularity, expanded the idea of the influence of shape to architecture. Martin vividly outlines how Fowler proposed this new house structure and publicized it in *A Home for All, or A New, Cheap, Convenient, and Superior Mode of Building (1848)*. With 8 walls, windows on all sides, a central staircase, an octagon house was more efficient, increased light and better air circulation.

Praising the efficacy of its design, Fowler saw plain, unadorned octagon houses as accessible for both wealthy and ordinary families. He eschewed Victorian ostentation, finding elegance in simplicity and, in subsequent editions, advocated the novel use of concrete as a building material. Fishkill, New York was the site of his own octagon.

For the next twenty years, over 2000 octagon houses were built throughout the United States and Canada. There was even a plan for 'Octagon City' in Kansas for a vegetarian colony.[iii] Only the American Civil War put the brakes on octagon house construction.

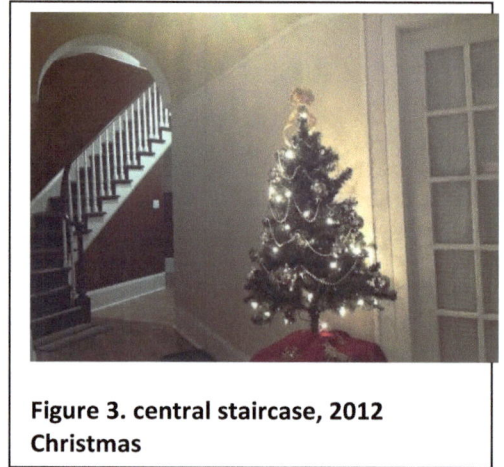

Figure 3. central staircase, 2012 Christmas

As for Fowler, financial setbacks aside, he pushed the envelope a tad too far in his later writings that led to his dying in obscurity. People could be intrigued by his advocacy for women's rights and distain for child labour, but publishing a sex manual was too much.

Unlike phrenology, Fowler's advocacy of octagon houses have gained respect

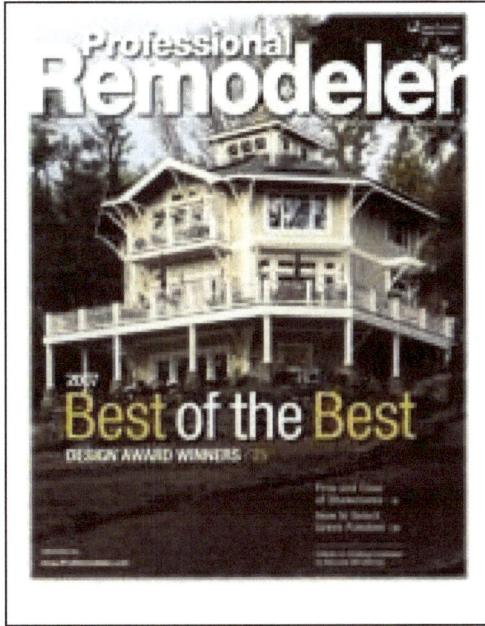

and appreciation lately, example being the article by Heins for the New York Times Service. [iv] An example of the avant-garde green build world, Sylvain Côté, Quebec native and president of Absolute Green Homes in South Salem, New York State, renovated a 1980s octagon house as a green building – see the 2007 award-winning transformation online. [v] Allen Dusault of Sustainable Conservation wrote about the energy efficiency and green footprint of an octagonal design over cookie-cutter rectangular house plans. [vi]

Ellen Puerzer and Robert Kline are the authorities of octagon houses still standing. In 2011, she published the definitive resource, *The Octagon House Inventory*. His internet site on octagon houses is at http://www.octagon.bobanna.com/main_page.html

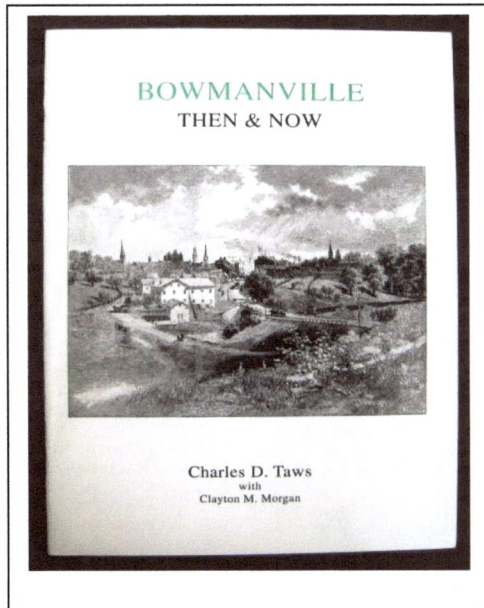

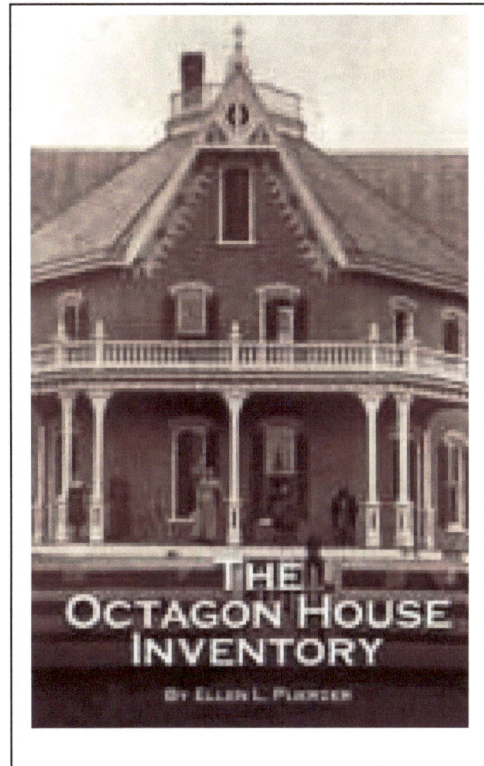

6   The Canadian Statesman, Bowmanville. July 27, 1977

Unique Octagon House Was Built in 1864

By Fred Cane, Bowmanville

The Octagon on 48 Division St. was built in 1864 for the trustees of the Congregational Church. It served as their parsonage for over twenty-five years. A Congregational Church has opened in Bowmanville as early as 1840 with Rev. T. Machin as the first minister. However in 1855. Rev. Thomas Reikie, a Scottish immigrant, became their minister and it was he and his family who were the first occupants of the Octagon. Reikie was succeeded in 1874 by Rev. Allworth who held the position for only one year, and then by Rev. W.H. Heu de Bourck, whose wife was said to be a German baroness. They were followed by Rev. William Warriner who was minister between 1882 and 1890. During his pastorate the Congregational Church was destroyed by fire and replaced by a beautiful brick building

which stood on the present site of the Canadian Tire Store.

After 1890 the Congregational Church declined and in 1900 the Octagon was sold to Henry Tait one of Bowmanville's early photographers. In 1905 it became the home of Mr. and Mrs. Archibald Tait. Archie Tait was a well known grocer and he became mayor in 1905. After Mrs. Tait's death, the Octagon became the property of her nephew, Mr. Mack Irwin of Port Hope. Mr. Irwin has owned the house since 1946.

The Octagon is a building unique in Bowmanville and is one of a small number of such houses in Ontario, most of which were built during the 1850's. Furthermore, because of its location, it forms part of an important grouping of four mid-nineteenth century houses, all situated at the intersection of Division and Wellington Streets. Constructed of brick, the Octagon is

covered with smooth stucco. The stucco was originally lined to imitate cut stone, a not common method of finishing stucco during the mid-nineteenth century. Some of these incised lines can still be seen on the north and east sides of the house. The front door is surmounted by a rectangular transom with sidelights and the windows retain their original sash. The square tower on the roof may at one time have contained two small windows which would have brought light into the central stairwell. The tall finial of the roof of the tower originally was flanked by two equally tall chimneys, similar to those on Colborne Lodge, High Park, Toronto. Early photographs show the house with louvred shutters and indicate that the house did not originally have a veranda. The

present veranda was added during the first decade of this century.

Notes: The 1864 date for the building of the Octagon has been determined by an examination of the assessment rolls for the period 1857-1867, which show an appreciable increase in value between 1863 and 1865. Furthermore, this date coincides with the purchase of the property by the Congregational Church on May 5, 1864 for only $5.00. Other references: Bowmanville, A Retrospect, 1958, pp. 60,61,80; the Townships of Darlington and Clarke, John Squair, 1927, pp. 313-315; The 1958 Centennial edition of the Canadian Statesman; the 1888 insurance map and an early photograph in the Bowmanville Museum; the 1861 Census of the Town of Bowmanville.

ENNISKILLEN

Figure 4. Fred Crane article, Canadian Statesman, July 27, 1977

Chapter 2. Bowmanville's 8-Sided Parsonage

THE CANADIAN STATESMAN, BOWMANVILLE, ONTARIO

Pedagogues of Early Days in Bowmanville's Many Schools

By D. Morrison. Sr.

Figure 5. Canadian Statesman, Mar 25, 1937

The site of the Octagon House of course was originally First Nations territory although I could not track down more archival information than that. William Humber's *Bowmanville: Small Town at the Edge*[vii] provides a details of the town's early history.

From the March 25, 1937 article 'Pedagogues of Early Day in Bowmanville's Many Schools', journalist D Morrison Sr writes that a 'Mrs Geo Reed ran a private school on Division Street about where Mr Tod had his bake shop, afterwards the octagon house now owned by Mrs Archie Tait.' There may be more information about what other buildings had been on the property that predated the actual octagon building itself.

The Congregational Church opened in 1840 with the Rev T Machin as minister on land donated by Charles Bowman of Montreal[viii]. J. B. Fairburn mentions in his *History of Bowmanville*, Reverend John Climio, a US evangelist, held a series of meetings at the Congregational Church[ix]. (It was known as Trinity Congregational Church, not to be confused with current Trinity United Church, which only took on its present name in 1925 – before that, it was known as the Methodist Church or Church Street Methodist Church.) The church built a manse for resident clergy.

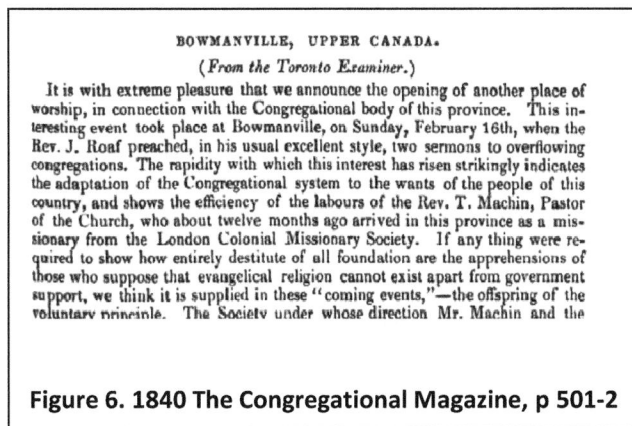

BOWMANVILLE, UPPER CANADA.
(*From the Toronto Examiner.*)
It is with extreme pleasure that we announce the opening of another place of worship, in connection with the Congregational body of this province. This interesting event took place at Bowmanville, on Sunday, February 16th, when the Rev. J. Roaf preached, in his usual excellent style, two sermons to overflowing congregations. The rapidity with which this interest has risen strikingly indicates the adaptation of the Congregational system to the wants of the people of this country, and shows the efficiency of the labours of the Rev. T. Machin, Pastor of the Church, who about twelve months ago arrived in this province as a missionary from the London Colonial Missionary Society. If any thing were required to show how entirely destitute of all foundation are the apprehensions of those who suppose that evangelical religion cannot exist apart from government support, we think it is supplied in these "coming events,"—the offspring of the voluntary principle. The Society under whose direction Mr. Machin and the

Figure 6. 1840 The Congregational Magazine, p 501-2

Bowmanville experienced a building boom in the 1850's due to the Grand Trunk Railway, later part of the CPR, a time of construction of the houses at the Wellington/Division historic four-corners, 86 Wellington (by Marshall Porter, 1858), Waltham's Cottage (1852), John McClung House (1858), the Octagon House (1864).

The Congregational magazine [formerly The London Christian Instructor].

502   *Transactions of the Congregational Churches,*   July,

brethren in this Province are labouring, is entitled to the gratitude and patronage of every friend to religious liberty. We augur that the Society will not only realize their expectations with regard to the diffusion of the Gospel, but ultimately there will be secured to us the establishment of principles that will constitute our safeguard against oppressive hierarchies, and secure to every man his right of exercising a spontaneous liberality in the support of the cause of Christ, The Chapel of Bowmanville is of gothic character—neat in exterior and chastely fitted up within. It is the result of much taste, and the architect has evidently done it—*con amore.* The land was handsomely presented by C. Bowman, Esq. of Montreal. The collection amounted to more than £20.

Fred Crane did some detective work in the assessment rolls. The property was purchased for $5.00 by the Congregational Church on May 5, 1864, with its value increasing between 1863 and 1864. Based on this, Fred Cane concluded in a long article in the Canadian Statesman, July 27, 1977, the date of 1864 when the octagon took shape. Given that the Orson Squires Fowler was influential in the Burned Out District of western New York where Congregationalist churches were extremely active, this might explain why this church decided on such a unique design for the manse.

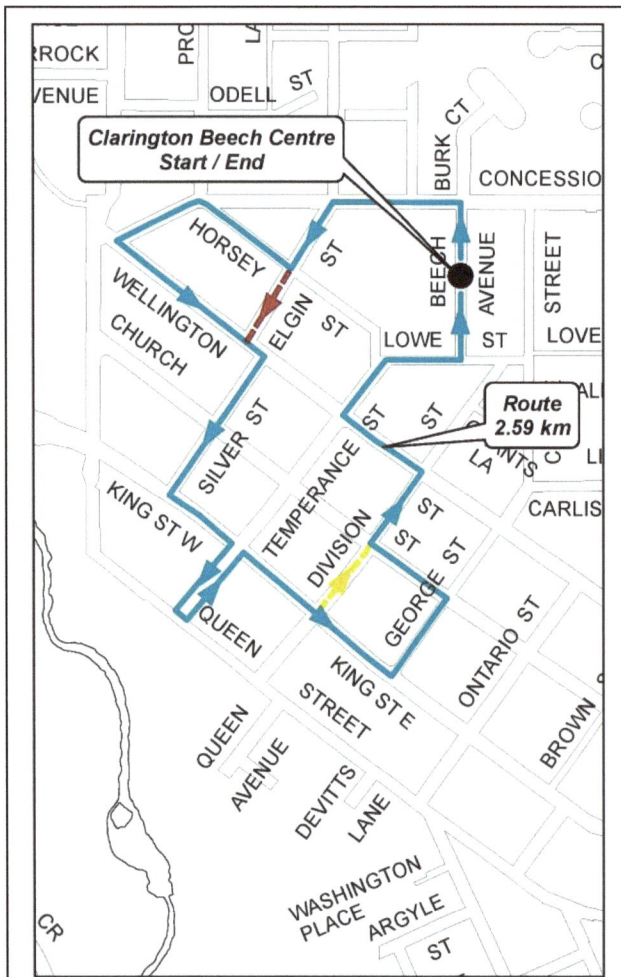

Bowmanville's Octagon House is topped by a square cupola. From up there, at the time of construction, the view from the belvedere would have been an unobstructed view to Lake Ontario as all the buildings on present day King Street were not yet there.

For the next 36 years, the resident clergy included:

1855 – 1874 The Rev Thomas Miller Reikie and his 1st wife Margaret, then 2nd wife Marion
1874 – 1875 The Rev Allworth
1875 – 1881 The Rev W. H. Heu de Bourck
1882 – 1890 The Rev William Henry Warriner[x]
1891 – The Rev Magee Pratt [xi]
1892 – 1895 The Rev W. S. Pritchard[xii]
1897 – 1899 The Rev J. H. Barnett

Figure 5. Walking Tour of Historic Bowmanville. ClaringtonHeritage.ca

The manse was popular for church meetings and music recitals.

The Reverend Thomas Reikie left his congregation in Bowmanville rather abruptly after almost 20 years at the church. Jill Downie of *A Passionate Pen* notes that there was a marked absence of the usual flowery farewells. The widowed middle-aged childless Rev Reikie's remarriage to Marion, a young Montreal woman in her early 20s, sparked comment amongst his congregation. In any event, a son from this marriage later took holy orders, The Rev T Thomson Reikie.

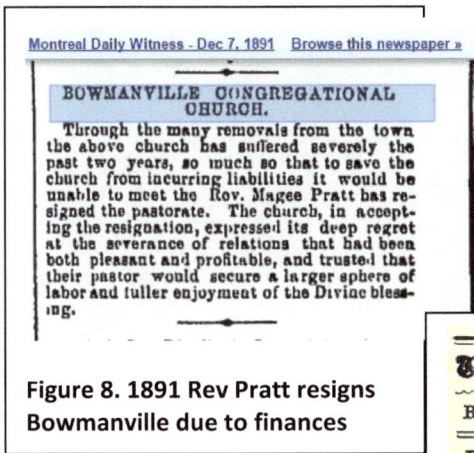

Figure 8. 1891 Rev Pratt resigns Bowmanville due to finances

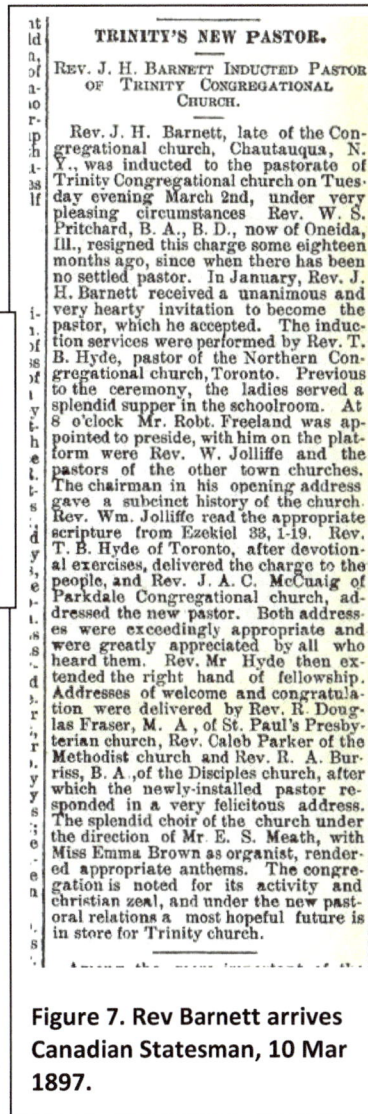

Figure 6. Reikie family stone

Figure 7. Rev Barnett arrives Canadian Statesman, 10 Mar 1897.

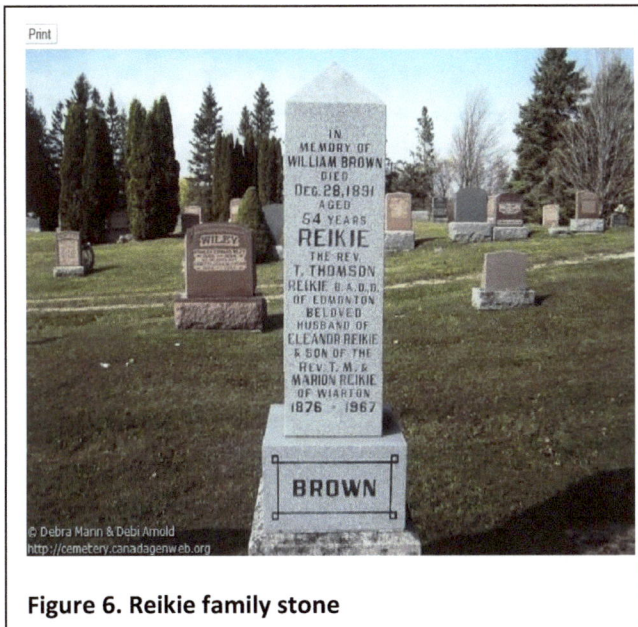

Courtesy Clarington Museums and Archives". and Janice Seto

Located at 48 Division Street, this house represents an architectural style that is rare in Ontario. The eight-sided octagon design was promoted by an eccentric American, named Orson Squire Fowler, in the 1850s. Essentially, Mr. Fowler felt that a traditional house, where items piled up unhandily in the corners, caused bad temperament among the occupants. They, in turn, soured the temperament of their children "*Thus rendering the whole family bad dispositioned by nature*" as he lamented in his book about the virtues of octagon buildings.

Mr. Fowler's concepts were never enthusiastically taken up by the masses, but a small number of octagonal houses, barns, and even outhouses, were built in Ontario. This example was constructed in 1864 as a parsonage for the Trinity Congregational Church (part of this church building can be seen in our Present Home Hardware Store). The Congregational Minister, Mr. Thomas Reike, was the first occupant. Other ministers who lived here include Rev. Allworth, Rev. W.H. Heu de Bourck (whose wife was said to be a German Baroness), and Rev. William Warriner.

This picture shows later resident Archibald Tait and his family on the front porch. Mr. Tait was mayor of Bowmanville in 1905-1906, and ran a grocery store on the main street (present day location of the Coronation Restaurant). He purchased the house from his brother, H.C. Tait. Henry Clay Tait was a well known photographer in town before he emigrated to Alberta in 1905 and died there in 1929.

In 1946, Mack Irwin, a nephew of Mrs. A. Tait, owned the house and converted it into apartments.

Pre 1900 photo with original wooden stairway which predates the later 3 sided verandah.

Figure 11. Picture The Way We Were: A Pictorial History of Darlington & Clarke Townships, 1980, p 182

Figure 10. Rev Barnett will reside Octagon - Canadian Statesman, 10 Feb 1897

Figure 12. Last sermon Rev Barnett Canadian Statesman, 15 Feb 1899

Figure 9. Canadian Statesman, 10 Sep 1936.

It appears Trinity Congregational Church struggled for worshippers – and eventually the church sold the Octagon House in 1900 to Henry Tait, photographer and his wife and 9 children.

Photographer Henry Tait bought the Octagon house from the Church in 1900 but with a move to Edmonton planned, sold the building to brother Archie Tait in 1905. It became the property of Mrs. Tait's nephew, Mack Irwin, in 1946. When the Taits lived there they took in boarders. This foreshadowed what was to come: in recent years the Octagon has been an apartment dwelling, managed by Henry Irwin of Port Hope.

Figure 13. Picture The Way We Were: A Pictorial History of Darlington & Clarke Townships, 1980 p 182

Figure 14. June 23, 1897 – Canadian Statesman 1937

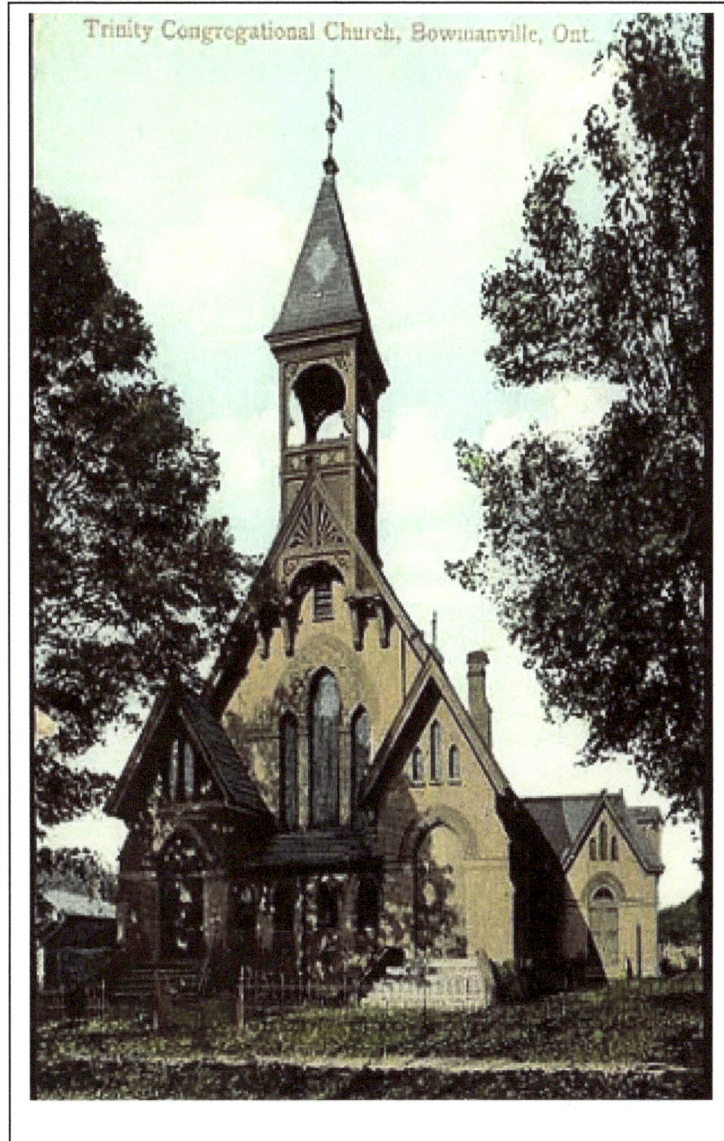

Trinity Congregational Church, Bowmanville, Ont.

Chapter 3. Writing Became Faith Fenton

You can write a book about Alice Freeman, the journalist known by her pen name of Faith Fenton… actually, that book has been written by Jill Downie, the historian and mystery writer.

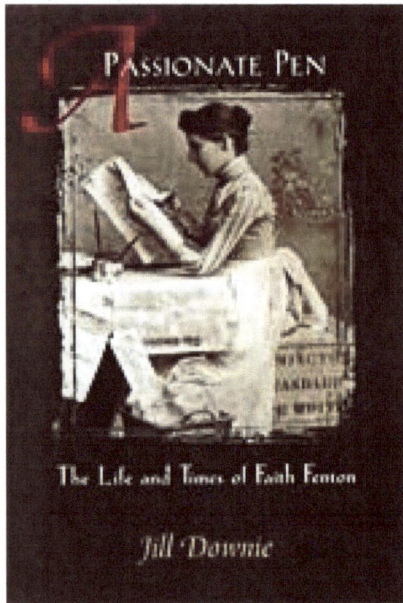

A Passionate Pen: The Life & Times of Faith Fenton was shortlisted for Governor General's Award, for Non-Fiction in 1996 and won the **Drummer General's Award** by A Different Drummer Books in Burlington, Ontario. Ms Downie conducted extensive research in Bowmanville for this book. Her insights as to the social life in Bowmanville, Liberals vs Tory, and church life lend these early years of the town a certain depth that may be lacking in strictly historical narratives.

Figure 15. A Passionate Pen: The Life & Times of Faith Fenton by Jill Downie

Alice Freeman was born in Bowmanville in 1857 to a rather large family that later moved north of Toronto. At age ten, due to family financial difficulty, young Alice was sent in 1867 to live with the Scottish immigrant, the Reverend Thomas Reikie, and his wife, Margaret, in Bowmanville. Mrs Reikie, having no children of her own, taught music[xiii] and supervised Alice's four years going to the Union School, the site of today's Central Public School, wrote poetry.

Alice later trained as a teacher and led a double life in order to supplement her income. Getting half the pay of a male teacher, she took up journalism to make ends meet, under the pseudonym of Faith Fenton. If anyone had known it was Miss Freeman who was out at all hours investigating crimes against women, poverty in Toronto, etc, she would have lost her teaching job.

Jill Downie, a member of the Writers Union of Canada, http://www.writersunion.ca/member/jill-downie is interviewed here:

http://www.openbooktoronto.com/news/ten_questions_with_jill_downie

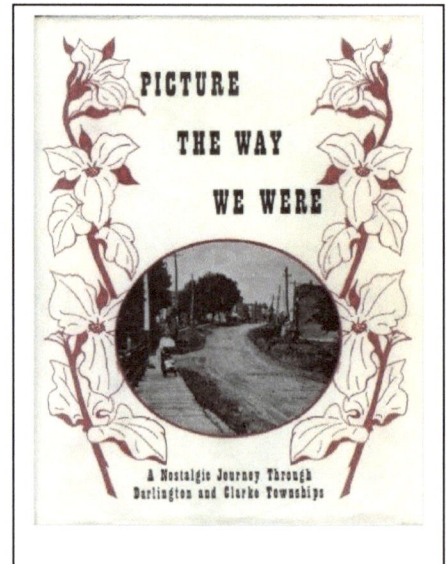

Ms Downie later travelled to Guernsey to write the Moretti/Falla mystery series, and preparing more followup novels in the series.

Faith Fenton's story has inspired Rosemary Rowe to write "Camp Victoria". Fenton is a lead character in the Lunchbox Theatre 2014 production of historical comedy, directed by Rosemary Rowe. This is partially based on the Faith Fenton columns she wrote as an intrepid reporter in the Yukon. Lindsay Burns as Fenton was nominated for 2014 Calgary Critics Award.[xiv]

Alice Freeman is buried in Toronto. Ironically, after she passed and just like Margaret Reikie, her widower, Dr John Brown, married someone much younger, in this case, Olivia Freeman, Alice's much younger niece. [xv]

Figure 16. Grave of Alice Freeman, 'Faith Fenton' at Mount Pleasant Cemetery, Toronto

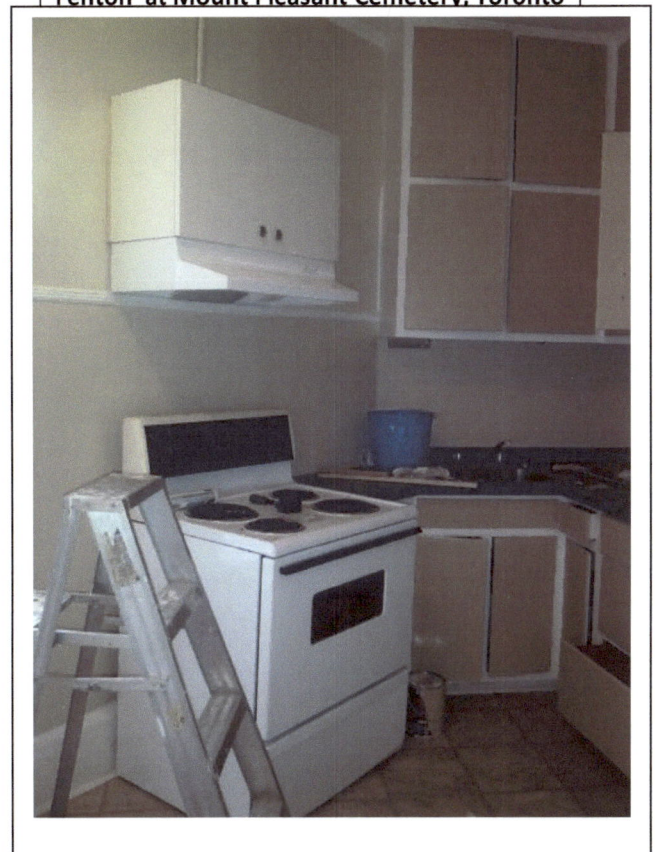

Chapter 4. Tait The Photographer

7-6ins.

THE
Looking Glass
ECLIPSED!

We the undersigned, would respectfully inform the public, that we have

Purchased the entire

Photographic Business,

formerly carried on by E. & H. O'HARA, and MR. HENRY, and would say to all, that we have

First-class Facilities
for making
First-class Work.

We keep on hand, a Good Stock of

ALBUMS & FRAMES,

of Various Styles and Prices.

We would also remind those who wish

GOOD PHOTOS',

to not spend the day in shopping, and when fatigued, suddenly determine to be Photographed. If you do it is sure to be a failure.

EXTRA PAINS
taken to procure
GOOD PICTURES OF CHILDREN.

Be sure to Come Early; In the fore part of the day; Especially with the BABIES

Business hours from 9 a. m. till 4 p. m., during the Winter months.

HARRY TAIT. JAS. ARTHUR

AT THE NEW GALLERY.

Prints can be had of all negatives taken in O'Hara's and Henry's Galleries, and also prints from negatives taken in Fletcher's Gallery by H. Tait.

Bowmanville, Nov. 12th, 1873. hp-o43-md-tf.

Figure 17. Henry C Tait photographer, Merchant And General Advertiser (Bowmanville, 28 Nov 1873)

Henry Clay Tait, local photographer, ran several studios over the years in Bowmanville and the surrounding area (c. 1870s to 1905). He is one of the sons of George Tait and his wife, who owned land in the area courtesy of the 1847 purchase by his father, John Tait. The history of the Taits, the Smarts, and the Soper family is partially presented below in this Statesman article.

Henry C Tait and his wife and 9 children appear to have lived in the Octagon House from 1900 to 1905. In the summers, they headed to the shore of Lake Ontario until school started again. The Shaw Photograph Collection of the Clarington Museum and Archives feature 'Camp Chatter', the name the Tait family gave to their tent city camp on Bowmanville beach. Apparently, other people then followed, building cottages and summer homes in what became Port Bowmanville.

1957 THE CANADIAN STATESMAN, BOW

Dates Back to 1846

Land Purchased by J. & J. Steeped in Local History

The land which has been purchased by Johnson & Johnson Limited on which to erect a new plant here is bound up in the history of Bowmanville. The 34 acres includes parts of the Soper and Short farms, dating back to the early days of this district. These farms were owned by David Smart and John Smart respectively, the deed of the Soper property coming from the Crown to David Smart on Jan. 24, 1846.

David and John Smart were brothers who came from Dundee, Scotland, and there was as well another brother, George, who J. B. Fairbairn records in his "History and Reminiscenes of Bowmanville," came to Bowmanville to succeed his father, Robert Fairbairn, in the management of the Bowman business but was only in charge a short time. He was killed in an accident, and his wife dying shortly afterward, his two children were adopted, one by David Smart at Port Hope, and the other by John Smart at Darlington.

Soper Farm

John Smart was one of the original shareholders and directors of the Port Darlington Harbour Company, formed in 1839, and we believe that David Smart was an early shareholder in the Port Hope Harbour Company. The land, known as the Soper farm, which David Smart received from the Crown, in all 160 acres at that time, he did not keep long, selling the north 93 acres to John Tate or Tait in July 2, 1847, and the south 60 acres to F. W. Gates and John Simpson on Jan. 21, 1851. John Simpson was one of the town's most illustrious citizens, rising from a clerk in the Bowman business to be the founder of the Ontario Bank in 1857, and was made a Senator in 1867.

It is the north part of the farm which is concerned in the present enterprise, and from this John Tait sold to the Grand Trunk Railway Company in November, 1854, about 2½ acres.

The northern section came into the Soper family in May 16, 1885, by a deed from George Tait to George Washington Soper. This portion of the extensive lands owned in early days by the Soper family, pioneers in this district, was in the Township of Darlington and has recently been annexed by the Town of Bowmanville.

Old Families

The Sopers and Taits are both well known old families. Leonard Soper was a United Empire Loyalist who migrated from Vermont in the United States to Prince Edward County in Canada in 1788. His wife was one of the Marsh family which took up a large grant of land in Hope Township. The Sopers joined the Marsh's there in 1795, but while in Prince Edward County, their son Timothy was born, said to be the first white child born in Sidney Township.

In 1805 Leonard Soper moved to Darlington and built the first saw mill in the township. In 1806 he bought land in Lot 9, of the town, above the Base Line, from Augustus Barber and here erected a flour mill. For many years past, this mill has been known as McKay's Mill where the famous Cream of Barley was produced. The Sopers owned lands in Clarke Township as well.

Taits of Octagon

Montreal Plant - A Busy Place

Figure 18. Tait Family of early 1840s Bowmanville (Feb 28, 1957 Cdn Statesman)

Township as well.

Taits of Octagon

The George Tait from whom George Washington Soper purchased the Darlington Township property, now to be part of the Johnson & Johnson premises, was the father of Archie Tait, a well known grocer whose store was where the Coronation Cafe is now. Another son was Harry Tait, a photographer, who prior to moving to Edmonton lived in the Octagon house on the corner of Division and Wellington Streets. Archie Tait also occupied the Octagon later. There are many Bowmanville and ex-Bowmanville residents who remember shopping in Archie Tait's and remember Bobby Holmes who was associated with him.

The Soper farm has been occupied for the past number of years by Clarence Soper.

Short Farm

The Taits of the Octagon hosted socials with music as found in the pages of the Canadian Statesman.

Henry Tait and his wife and their 9 children appeared to have owned the Octagon for only 5 years, making their intention to leave in 1905 for Edmonton. He sold the property to his brother, Archie Tait, and L A W Tole hosted an auction on Sept 9, 1905 to sell all.(Aug 30, 1905 of the Statesman.)

AUCTION SALE.

SATURDAY, SEPT. 9—Mr. H C. Tait will sell all of his household furniture and furnishings at his residence, 'The Octagon,' Division St , Bowmanville Sale at 1 p.m. See bills. L A. W. TOLE, auctioneer.

Aug 19, 1948, Jack Tait from Medicine Hat, Alberta paid his first visit to Bowmanville and the Octagon House, he is the son of Albert Tait and his wife, born Marie Matthews of Kendal.

ard Witheridge have returned home after a pleasant motor trip to Ottawa and Hull. While there, they spent several days in Eastview visiting Mr. and Mrs. Ernest Hunt.

Mr. and Mrs. Raymond Meads, Toronto, daughter Barbara, 15, recently chosen Beaches Beauty Queen, and son, Neville, 8, were Sunday visitors with Mr. Alfred Shrubb and Miss Nancy Shrubb. Mr. Meads is president, Gladstone Athletic Club.

Mr. and Mrs. H. J. Babcock spent a few days in Toronto last week as guests at the La Plaza Hotel, when Mr. Babcock was a delegate to the Supreme Lodge, S. O. E., B.S. Convention which was held for three days in the roof garden of the Royal York Hotel.

From its inception the Canadian National Exhibition has emphasized educational features, particularly those departments appealing most to school children. More than six hundred thousand school children in the Province of Ontario are invited each year to be the guests of the directors. Each receives a personal invitation to be present.

The editor of The Statesman was pleased to receive a call on Tuesday from Mr. John M. Tait, B.S., B.Ed., Medicine Hat, Alta.

Jack is a high school teacher, born in Edmonton and was paying his first visit to eastern Canada and expressed himself as most favorably impressed with Ontario. He is a son of Albert H. Tait of Edmonton, Alta., who was born in Bowmanville, and grandson of Harry C. Tait who carried on a successful photography business in this town for many years before the turn of this century when the Tait family went west. Jack had the satisfaction of seeing the house in which the Taits lived, "The Octagon," corner of Wellington and Division Sts., as he had often heard his father speak of the unusual architecture of this house. He also had the pleasure of seeing Dr. Norman Allin who lived for many years in Edmonton and is now living in town.

West Beach News

(The Beach Comber)

The Beach Association met on Sunday morning and plans are underway to provide the kiddies with a movie on Sunday evening.

A euchre will be held at Mrs. Fred Cole's on Thursday evening.

On Saturday, August 21, a huge weiner roast will be given to all

Figure 19. Albert Tait visits - Canadian Statesman, 26 Jul 1961

entered vehicles of | shows the finish with the Franklin Park

Former Resident Notes Many Improvements Here Since He Left 60 Yrs. Ago

By Dr. Geo. W. James

Mr. and Mrs. Albert H. Tait, son school master John Tait and grandson Fraser Tait, all from Edmonton, Alta., have been renewing old acquaintances in Mr. Tait Sr.'s native town of Bowmanville which he left nearly 60 years ago.

This is only the second time he has returned here for a visit and he noted many improvements since he lived here, particularly paved streets, waterworks and sewage system, modern hospital with large addition now under construction, population more than doubled with hundreds of new homes built on what were cow pastures and fields in his boyhood days.

He was also favorably impressed with the up-to-date appearance of the attractive stores along King St. Quite different, he remarked before the turn of the century, when he was a clerk in the grocery store of his uncle, ex-mayor

Archie Tait, where the Coronation Cafe is now located.

Older citizens will also recall way back in the 80's when Albert's father, Harry C. Tait, had his photographic studio in the Horsey Block where Owen Nicholas' Barber Shop is now located on Temperance St. Those were the days when it was quite the style for many families to have a group photo of mother, father and the children, decked out in their Sunday-go-meeting best clothes, prominently displayed in the plush family album in the parlor to proudly show visitors. Even today, eighty years and more later, these family groups taken by "H. C. Tait, Photographer" are found in the homes of many of our pioneer families, on to the fourth generation, still living here.

Of a family of nine children of the Harry Tait family born in Bowmanville, only four are still living, all residing in Western Canada, Cas-

(TURN TO PAGE SEVEN)

New School Boun Set Up by Distric

The Board met July 19th in Millbrook. In the absence of the Chairman, Mr. Reg. Fallis, past Chairman presided.

A resignation from the Board, for health reasons, was read from Fred Lycett of Or-

vious meeting to prepare a recommendation as to boundaries for each high school (the Board felt that the time had come to set up regulations governing the school which students may attend.)

Figure 20. Albert Tait visits, Canadian Statesman (Bowmanville, ON), 26 Jul 1961

Former Resident

(FROM PAGE ONE)

sell, Albert, Preston and John. The family will be remembered by many old citizens when it is recalled "Oh, they are the Taits who lived in the Octagon House, corner of Wellington and Division Sts.," now converted into an apartment building.

It should be mentioned that Albert's wife who accompanied them on this trip was Marie Matthews, native of Kendal. They were married 52 years ago. She therefore qualifies as a member of that illustrious sons and daughters of Durham County.

The Statesman must get in a "plug" in this historical sketch by mentioning that the Taits through the years have kept well informed on what has been going on back in Bowmanville and dear old Durham County by being subscribers to "Durham County's Great Family Journal."

MISS MABEL A. TAIT,

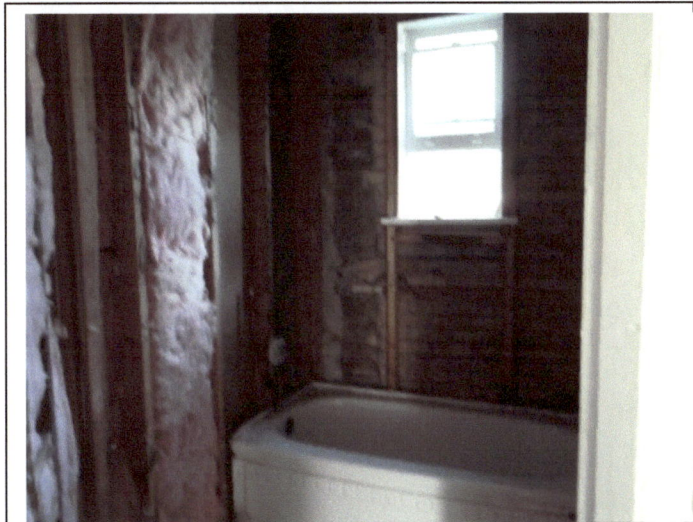

GOLD MEDALIST—and Fellow of Toronto College of Music and late Organist and Choir Director of Yonge St. Methodist Church, Toronto, is prepared to take a limited number of pupils in voice (Soprano only) Piano and Theory. Pupils prepared for Musical examinations at Toronto University, Toronto Conservatory of Music and Toronto College of Music. Apply between 9 a.m. and 5 p.m. at Tait & Co's Studio. Evenings at "The Octagon" corner Wellington and Division Sts., Bowmanville. Terms moderate.

Figure 21. Music lessons at the Octagon, Statesman, 22 Mar 1905, p. 4

Good Things For Picnic Hampers

The picnic is a pleasant and favorite form of summer entertainment with both old and young. The lunch, however, is an important factor in the successfulness of the outing. We will give some suggestions that probably will help you. Try Minced Meat Sandwiches, two-thirds chopped ham and one-third tongue, mixed together with mayonnaise dressing, spread on white bread with lettuce leaves.

OLIVES

Don't forget to include some appetizing Olives and Pickles, also

Summer Drinks to Quench Your Thirst

FANCY BISCUITS

Are easy to carry and are tasty and satisfying. We have a a nice assortment.

RUBBER JAR RINGS

See that you get a new lot for preserving time. Let us fill your next grocery order.

ARCHIE TAIT

Phone 65   Bowmanville

Figure 22. Archie Tait advertisement, July 9, 1925, Canadian Statesman

Chapter 5. Tait The Retailer & Mayor

Henry Clay Tait sold the Octagon House to his widower brother, grocery store owner, Archie Tait. Already middle-aged, Archie soon married Hanna Aurilla McNall of Port Hope in 1906. By then, he was already serving as Mayor.

June 21, 1955, page 6. "In the Dim and Distant Past from the Statesman Files": 49 years ago (1906) — Among the June weddings was that of Mayor Archie Tait and Miss Aurilla McNall of Port Hope.

PAGE SIX

In the Dim and Distant Past

From The Statesman Files

25 YEARS AGO (1930)

B. H. S. Screech Owl made its appearance for 1929-30. Miss E. M. Stedman was Consulting Editor. The contents were highly praised. One notices how much more important the literary side, encouraging the writing of poems and short stories, was then. Class room humor seems to have changed very little however, and sports, cartoons, and snapshots all played an important part in this edition of the old school magazine.

Ed. Witheridge and Ralph Ames, Sr., cleaned up all the prizes in horseshoe pitching at Columbus, winning against some of the best "shoe-tossers" in the district.

Number of electric signs making their appearance on King Street was worthy of note. W. J. Bagnell of the Grand Central being the latest to add an attractive Neon sign.

At a meeting at Orono, Fred W. Bowen was unanimously chosen as Conservative candidate in the forthcoming Federal election.

Orono—Police Trustees placed the bell tower on the fire hall where the fire alarm bell was installed It is noted that this bell for half a century swung in the Bowmanville South Ward bell tower.

Newcastle—Mr. and Mrs. W. H. Pearce celebrated their 35th wedding anniversary with members of their family. Mrs. Ira F. Pearce made the lovely bride's cake and the bride made an equally excellent cake for the groom. The couple was married in Castleton. Their two younger sons, Howard and Ernest were at home with them on the farm.

49 YEARS AGO (1906)

Postmaster J. B. Fairbairn in the instalment of his History of Bowmanville tells of Col Cubitt often speaking of a bear being shot in the vicinity now intersected by Beech Ave., when he first came to Darlington. He also tells of the many well-built houses put up by James Heal, Sr.

W. W. Short had new potatoes from his garden on June 9th.

Trinity congregational Ladies' Aid were planning an ice cream social on the lawn of the church, with the Durham Rubber Co. Band furnishing music for the occasion. Ice cream and cake 10c, additional ice cream 5c.

T. J. Irving, English representative of the D. O. & P. Co., Liverpool, England, were visiting Mr. J. W. Alexander, President of the D.O. & P. Co., at "The Evergreens."

Among the June weddings was that of Mayor Archie Tait and Miss Aurilla McNall of Port Hope.

A grand reception was given the man who walked from Port Hope to Toronto, James Reynolds, on his return to Port Hope. Citizens' band headed a long procession through Port Hope.

C. W. Slemon, Haydon, passed his final examinations for M.D.C.M.

The Town was having trouble with the electric light system and Councillor Spry said he doubted if another town in Canada would tolerate the service we had here.

Mr. & Mrs. W. Rahm Honored on Their 30th Anniversary

Figure 23 Wedding of Mayor Archie Tait & Aurilla McNall, 1905

Tomato Catsup

To make a Catsup one that will keep. Try the following

Cut up one bushel of clean ripe tomatoes and add two pints of vinegar, one cupful of salt, eight large onions, (sugar if desired) and stew for two hours, then strain or pass through a fine sieve, mix a little cold water with half a cup of corn starch or flour and add to the strained tomatoes, simmer for two or three hours or until it is a suitable thickness and add a bottle of Lee's Catsup Flavor, mix thoroughly bottle and cork tightly while still hot. Lee's Catsup Flavor and Preserver saves time, labor and material prevents souring, produces a natural red colored Catsup of fine flavor.

25c a bottle

For sale only at

TAITS' GROCERY.

Figure 18. Tait's tomato catsup recipe, Canadian Statesman, 15 Aug 1906

The archives of the Canadian Statesman show Archie Tait grocery business (formerly of Crowker & Tait) regularly advertising items for sale and household tips, such as the recipe for 'tomato catsup'

As the owner of the Octagon House, he was responsible for the porch that covers 2 sides of the house, circa 1905 – 1910. From photos of the era, the porch originally contained a balcony on top with door leading out on the second floor. Seated with his wife, Archie Tait is joined by his nephew by marriage, Henry Luther McNall 'Mac' Irwin.

Ten years after he bought the Octagon House, and built the porch, the Statesman congratulated Archie Tait on giving the 50 year old residence a dab of paint. Yep, everyone notices…

This front-page lead story on the life of Archie Tait reminds the reader of the businessman and the politician who was active at St John's Anglican Church.

5c a Copy   No. 52

EX-MAYOR ARCHIE TAIT PASSES AFTER BRIEF ILLNESS

One of Bowmanville's life-long residents and leading business men has been called from active duty to a higher life in the person of Archibald Tait, grocer, who less than two weeks ago was at his place of business, meeting and serving his many friends and customers with his cheery smile and usual courtesy.

A short illness from flu and other complications baffled the skill of the medical men and he passed to rest on Sunday, December 23rd, aged 72 years.

Deceased was born near Port Bowmanville, being a son of the late Mr. and Mrs. George Tait, and nephew of the late Capt. Tait a well-known sailor of the Great Lakes half a century ago.

As a young man Archie, as he was familiarly called, kept a photograph gallery over England's bake shop on the corner of King and Division Streets, where the Balmoral Hotel now stands.

Several years he worked as clerk in the grocery store of the late John Milne, where the Bank of Commerce now stands. Later he went into business, the firm being known as Cawker & Tait, but for over 20 years now he has carried on the business himself in the present stand on King Street.

In a public way Mr. Tait has taken an active part in town affairs, serving as Councillor and Reeve and was Mayor of the town in 1905-1906. He was a Past President of the Chamber of Commerce; a member of the Canadian Club, and chairman of the Membership Committee.

He was a loyal supporter of the Conservative party, being honored with offices in local and county associations. In religion he was a valued member of St. John's Anglican Church, being a sidesman and member of the Parish Council and a former Warden.

He was a member of the Sons of Scotland, the Loyal Orange Lodge, and an Oddfellow, having completed fifty years' membership in Florence Nightingale Lodge, No. 66, I.O.O.F. on Dec. 4th, and was to have been presented with the 50-year Jewel next month. He was also a member of Jerusalem Lodge, A.F.&A.M. No. 31, G. R. C.

The funeral took place on Wednesday afternoon, service being conducted in St. John's Church by the Rector, Rev. R. J. Shires, assisted by two former Rectors of St. John's, Rev. T. A. Nind of Port Perry, and Rev. P. C. Muirhead, of Willowdale. Members of Jerusalem Lodge attended in a body and followed the remains to their last resting place in Welcome cemetery where Mr. F. C. Hoar, P.D.D.G.M., conducted the Masonic service at the grave.

Figure 26. Ex-Mayor Archie Tait passes away. Canadian Statesman, 27 Dec 1928.

In the Dim and Distant Past

From the Statesman Files

49 YEARS AGO
(May 20, 1915)

Mrs. (Rev.) E. A. Tonkin is visiting relatives in Toronto.

Miss Georgie Langmaid, Zion, recently visited friends in town.

Mr. Richard Philp, Nestleton, has purchased a new Ford auto.

Miss Elsie M. Bragg spent the weekend with Miss Edna Staples, Orono.

Mr. Albert B. Couch, of Montreal, Que., spent Sunday at his father's, Mr. W. B. Couch.

Mr. Archie Tait's residence, "The Octagon" has been much improved by a coat of paint.

Miss Lela Black, Scugog,

Figure 24. Archie Tait's Octagon House improved by paint job, May 20, 1915 issue Canadian Statesman

New Year Greetings

The close of another year has brought a very sad and sudden change in the management of this Old Reliable Grocery Store.

However, the staff takes this means of extending the Season's Greetings to the host of customers who have shared their patronage with this store during the year.

We hope the joyous Christmas Season brought you much happiness and that the New Year will bring you Success, Health and Happiness.

Archie Tait Estate,

Phone 65   Bowmanville

Figure 25 Season's Greetings shock that Archie Tait passed. Canadian Statesman, 27 Dec 1928.

First wife was Miss Janet Swan, and then Hanna Aurilla McNall, his widow. Survived by siblings, Mrs Tait's sister, Alfretta, and husband, Ebenezer Irwin, and her nephew and his wife, Mr and Mrs Mac Irwin.

Formerly a door out to now taken-down balcony, spring 2012

summer 2012

Newspaper column

Masonic service at the grave.

The pall-bearers were Messrs. C. A. Cawker, Harry Rice, T. A. Duston, A. L. Nicholls, M. W. Comstock and F. C. Palmer.

A great wealth of flowers from relatives, friends, business associates, lodges and church societies, testified to the esteem in which deceased was held, and sympathy for the bereaved.

Deceased was twice married, first to Miss Janet Swan, and secondly to Miss Hannah Aurilla (Lily) McNall, daughter of the late Luther N. McNall of Port Hope, who survives him; also two brothers, Mr. Harry C. Tait, Edmonton, Alta., and Mr. John Tait, Chicago, Ill., and one sister, Mrs. Chas. DeWilt, Chicago, Ill.

Among the relatives and friends present were: Dr. J. H. Elliott, Mr. Clarence Tait, Mr. Jos. Booth and daughter Marguerite, Mrs. Florence McCrimmon New, and Mr. John Wright, Toronto; Mr. and Mrs. Ebenezer Irwin, Mr. and Mrs. Mac Irwin, Port Hope; Mrs. Sandy Kelly and Miss Milligan, Cobourg; Mr. and Mrs. Harry Baskerville, Mr. and Mrs. James McBrien, Toronto; Mrs. E. M. Osborne, Toronto; and Mr. D. M. Tod, Oshawa.

All places of business were closed during the funeral service.

The floral tributes included: Pillow—Mrs. A. Tait; Baskets—Mrs. Delmage, Mr. and Mrs. Clarence S. Mason, Mr. and Mrs. W. H. Dustan and Mr. and Mrs. W. E. Gerry; Wreaths—Mr. and Mrs. Ewart Everson, Oshawa, A. F. & A. M., Mrs. Margaret DeWitt and family, Executive Chamber of Commerce, the Irwin family, Mr. and Mrs. Robert Holmes, L.O.L., W. H. Thickson and family, I.O.O.F.; Spray of roses— Mrs. R. B. Andrews, Miss M. M. Armour, Mrs. J. K. Galbraith and Mrs. Geo. B. McClellan; Sprays—W. P. Corbett, Thos. Dustan, Mr. New, Mr. Wright and Mrs. J. T. Gould, Mrs. Leigh-Mallory, Mr. Albert Colwill and family, Dr. Jabez H. Elliott and Grace, Toronto, Mr. and Mrs. W. L. McNall, Detroit, brother Harry, Albert and Mae, Mrs. E. Clarke and family, Mr. and Mrs. Harry Allin, Robt. R. Hoskin and daughters, St. John's Women's Auxiliary, Mr. and Mrs. Frank Jackman, Mr. and Mrs. John F. Cole, Jules Roenigk, National Grocers, Oshawa, Dr. and Mrs. R. W. Clark, brother John Tait, Mr. and Mrs. W. J. Culley, Mr. and Mrs. T. H. Knight, Mr. and Mrs. Geo. Richards, Mr. and Mrs. J. A. McClellan, Mr. and Mrs. Russell Williams, Mr. and Mrs. A. Mitchell, Mr. and Mrs. Percy Cowan, Mr. and Mrs. J. Lake Morden, Mr. and Mrs. J. Ross Stutt, Mr. and Mrs. W. H. Carruthers, Mr. and Mrs. T. Wes. Cawker, Mr. and Mrs. Sam Warner, Mrs. G. A. Edmondstone and Miss Dingman, Mr. and Mrs. Chas. M. Carruthers, M. A. James & Sons, Mr. and Mrs. Chas. Goodman, Mr. and Mrs. Fred Knox, Mr. and Mrs. F. C. Vanstone, Mr. and Mrs. C. M. Cawker and Addie, Rice & Co., Mr. Jas. Infantine.

Undated photos of the Octagon House with chimneys and garage

Figure 27. formerly Archie Tait Grocery store and later the Coronation Restaurant. 9 King Street West, Bowmanville

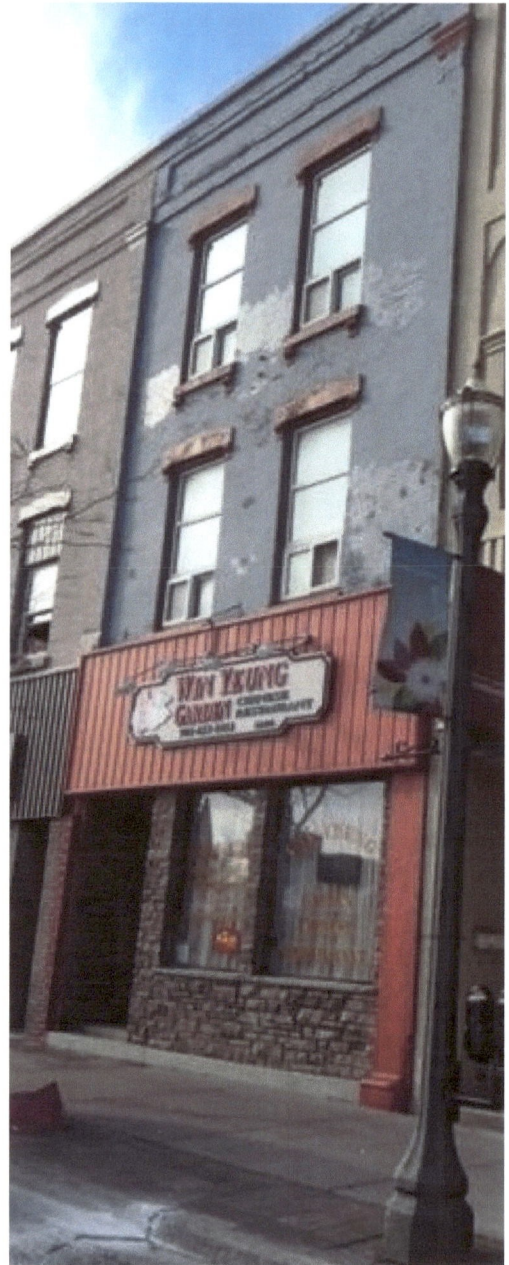

Figure 28. Bob Bate, Johnny Seto, back table, Coronation Restaurant c 1981

standalone tub
Octagon House

Chapter 6. Mrs Tait: 'Aunt Lil' of the McNalls, Port Hope

Mr Carmen Irwin mentioned that his great-aunt, Mrs Tait, was known to him as 'Aunt Lil'. It took me a few days of search to figure out that neither 'Lillian' nor 'Lilian' McNall of Port Hope could be found in the archives. Then I stumbled upon her real maiden name: Hanna McNall. Or more properly Hanna Aurilla McNall, hence Lil.

Figure 29 Anglican Women's Guild president Mrs Tait receives a piano lamp, Sept 13, 1923 Canadian Statesman

---

According to the Canadian Statesman obituary, January 4, 1945, Hanna Aurilla McNall was born in February 15, 1865 to the Luther McNalls the year after the Octagon house was built. From the announcement that Mayor Archie Tait married her in June 1906, I calculated that she was 41 and he was in his early 50s, probably why they had no children.

Some time after Archie Tait passed away, Mrs Tait closed the business and the premises were leased to the Coronation Café, which had been located across the road on the north-west side of the four corners of King and Temperance Streets.

TWENTY-FIVE YEARS AGO
September 13, 1923

Chas. F. Rice, Jas. Nokes and Hubert Foster were successful exhibitors in poultry at Toronto Exhibition.

About 30 members of the Woman's Guild, choir and others of St. John's Anglican Church, assembled at "The Octagon," the home of Mrs. Archie Tait, President of the Guild, and presented her with a beautiful piano lamp.

A most daring robbery was perpetrated at Courtice when John Walter, Postmaster and Storekeeper ,was robbed of about $200.

Solina—A pleasant social family gathering was held at the home of Mr. and Mrs. A. J. Reynolds, Sept. 10, when the fiftieth anniversary of their marriage was fittingly celebrated.

Figure 30. Dec 28, Dec 21, 1944

DEATHS

TAIT—In Bowmanville, Dec. 21, 1944,. Hannah Aurilla Tait, widow of Archibald Tait, in her 80th year.

JOLL—At Newcastle on December 21, 1944, Ada Mahala Potter, beloved wife of George H. Joll, aged 75 years. Interment Hampton Cemetery.

KING—At Bowmanville, on Sunday, December 17, 1944, James Arthur, infant son of Mr. and Mrs. Clary King, aged 2½ months. Interment Bowmanville Cemetery. 52-1*

Mrs Tait was quite active in St John's Anglican Church, the oldest church in town. As this snippet states, she had been president of the Woman's Guild St John's Anglican Church, and was presented a piano lamp when the group met at the Octagon.

In the obituary, there is no mention of any members of the Decker side of her sister's family at the funeral, although the family of her Irwin sister were - Mr and Mrs McNall (Mac) Irwin with their children Thelma and Carmen were, plus also Mrs Mac Irwin's father, Mr Bruce Crossley, of Hope Township

---

Figure 31 Mrs Irwin donates a quilt from late Mrs Tait for Red Cross auction, March 1946 Canadian Statesman

---

THURSDAY, MARCH 15th, 1945

SOCIAL AND PERSONAL
Phone 663

Mrs. James Cully has received a cable announcing her husband's safe arrival overseas.

TAYLOR'S

Mrs. S. Snell and Mrs. A. Weir, Toronto, visited Mr. and Mrs. M. W. Comstock.

Mr. and Mrs. S. N. Casbourn and Mrs. Lee Wheeler, Toronto, spent the week-end with Mr. and Mrs. H. Casbourn.

Mr. Fred Hughes, Toronto, spent the week-end with Mrs. Hughes and Jimmie at Mrs. Geo. Pritchard's.

Lieut. Bruce Cameron, St. John's, Que., visited Mrs. Alex Cameron and his father, Mr. H. Cameron.

Mr. and Mrs. Ralph Rea, Portage la Prairie, Man., are guests of Mrs. F. F. Morris and other relatives.

Mr. and Mrs. Charles Werry and the Misses Wright, Oshawa,

Lieut. N|S Zenia Castoldi was guest of her sister, Mrs. Jim Deas.

Mr. B. H. Mortlock, Ottawa, was guest of Chief S. Venton and Mrs. Venton.

Miss Marion Hooper spent the week-end with Mrs. Wm. Close, Brockville.

Mr. and Mrs. R. A. Wright, Oshawa, were guests at Mr. Norman Wright's.

eron, prior to Sgt. Kirk's departure for his home in Vancouver on 36 days' leave.

Mr. and Mrs. W. Begley, Arleen and Bruce, spent Sunday with relatives in Toronto.

Bowmanville High School girls play two and maybe three games of basketball in Cobourg, Saturday. It is hoped that at least some fans will be on hand from town to cheer them on to victory.

Bowmanville business men are invited to a banquet at Genosha Hotel, Oshawa, Wednesday, March 21, at 6:30 p.m., which is being sponsored by Oshawa Chamber of Commerce. Russell T. Kelly, Hamilton, will speak on "The Decentralization of Industry and the value of a Board of Trade". All towns and cities within a radius of 60 miles of Oshawa are invited to send representatives. If you can attend advise Mayor C. G. Morris not later than Monday.

Red Cross is benefitting from local auction sales conducted by W. J. Challis. At the sale of the late Mrs. Archie Tait a quilt was contributed by Mrs. McNall Irwin, Hope Township, which W. F. Rickard, M.P., purchased at $35, proceeds being divided equally between Port Hope and Bowmanville Red Cross Societies. At M. J. Elliott's sale last Saturday he bought the quilt put up by Haydon War Workers, at $15, and immediately turned it over to the local Red Cross which was again auctioned and was knocked down to Mr. Stackarack at $17.00.

Figure 32 Aurilla McNall Tait obituary - Canadian Statesman (Bowmanville, ON), 4 Jan 1945, p. 6

MRS. ARCHIE TAIT

Hanna Aurilla McNall, wife of the late Archie Tait, died in Bowmanville Hospital, December 21. In failing health for two years, the deceased passed peacefully away after two months spent in hospital under expert care which failed to restore her declining strength.

Mrs. Tait was in her 80th year, having been born in Hope Township, Feb. 15, 1865, daughter of the late Mr. and Mrs. Luther McNall, who later lived in Port Hope. After her marriage to the late Archie Tait, she came to live in Bowmanville, where she since resided until her death.

A member of St. John's Anglican Church, Mrs. Tait took keen interest in church work and was identified for many years with charitable undertakings. Her husband, Ex-Mayor Archie Tait, was widely known as proprietor of a grocery business in the premises now occupied by the Coronation Cafe. After his death in 1926, his widow continued to live in the family residence, "The Octagon" and carried on her interest in community affairs until failing health confined her to her home.

The funeral was held from the Morris Funeral Chapel on Saturday, Dec. 23, with Canon C. R. Spencer officiating in the services attended by friends and relatives whose presence attested the esteem in which the deceased was held. Interment took place at Welcome Cemetery and the pallbearers were, Fred Pattinson, F. O. McIlveen, F. C. Hoar, H. Ormiston, J. McConnachie and Geo. W. James.

Among the friends and relatives at the funeral were, Mr. and Mrs. McNall (Mac) Irwin, Thelma and Carman, Mr. Bruce Crossley, Hope Township. Beautiful floral tributes were expressive of the sentiment of the community which mourns the passing of an esteemed and generous citizen.

Figure 34. Danny Danson, Johnny Seto in front of St John's Anglican, Bowmanville, 1961

Figure 33. St John's Anglican Church - incumbent rector, the Rev Christopher Greaves

Chapter 7. The Octagon Turns 100 - Mac, 'Mr McIrwin'

A nephew of Mrs Tait, 'Aunt Lil' nee Aurilla McNall (Cdn Statesman June 26, 1958, p 35), inherited the Octagon House in 1946. I used to call him Mr McIrwin, because that's what Dad always called his landlord. It was not until years later while trying to find his phone number in the Bell directory for Dad and failing utterly - 'there is no listing for McIrwin' - that he corrected me with the fact the surname is merely 'Irwin' and his first name is Mac. Which actually turned out to be half-true. His real name was Mr. Henry Luther McNall Irwin, also known as Mac.

Figure 35. Henry McNall 'Mac' Irwin with Aunt 'Lil' Tait and Uncle Archie Tait circa 1905 - 1910

Mr Mac Irwin's full name contains in a nutshell the history of both sides of his family, stretching back almost 200 years in Hope Township.

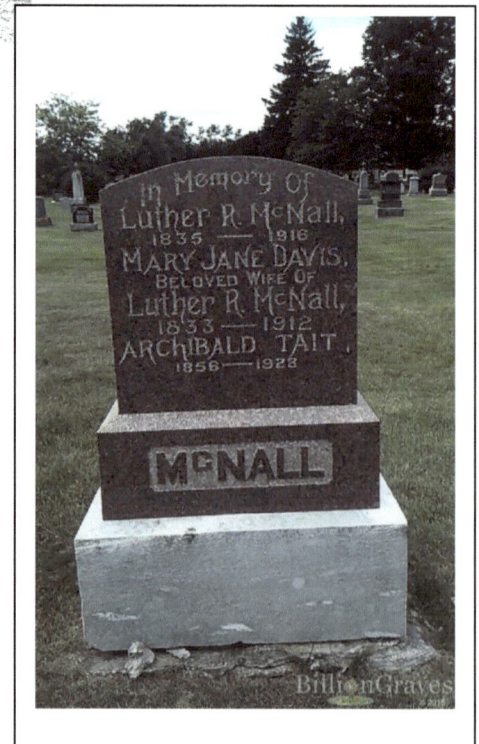

The Irwin family have lived in the former Hope Township for almost 200 years. From what I could find, the first Irwin in Canada was Irishman Dr John Taaffe Irwin (1799 – 1861). The son of Henry Jones Irwin and Hannah Taaffe, Dr Irwin came over to Upper Canada from County Sligo, Ireland and married in 1833 Lucinda Bradley, born 1806 Haldimand Township, died 1896 Hope Township. Their eldest son, Henry Jones Irwin (1834 – 1927) married Abigail Bedee (1832/5 – 1925), daughter of Ebenezer Bebee and Linda Vancura. Their eldest child and only son, Ebenezer Irwin (1861 – 1965) married Alfretta McNall of Port Hope (1862-1935).

008541-88, (Durham Co), Ebenezer GWIN, 26, Farmer, Hope Twp, same, s/o Henry & Abigail GWIN, married Alfarvetta **McNALL**, 25, Hope Twp, Port Hope, d/o Luther & Jane McNALL, Wtn Byron DECKER of Peterboro & Lilly McNALL of Port Hope, 22 Feb 1888 at Port Hope

Figure 36. Ebenezer Irwin marries Alfretta McNall, Feb 22, 1888 - Aurilla McNall witness p 3 Northumberland & Durham 1888 - scann

The McNall family of Port Hope, as far as I know, had been in Canada almost as long as the Irwins. Luther McNall (dates unknown) married Hannah Raymond (1808-1895) and had at least one child, Luther R McNall (1835-1916). Their son, Luther R McNall and his wife Mary Jane Davis McNall (1833-1912), had at least four daughters, Alfretta McNall Irwin (1862-1935), Hannah Aurilla McNall Tait (1864-1944), Rosanna B McNall (1867-1914), and Ameilla McNall (1868-?). It appears that of these four daughters, two remained spinsters. Hannah Aurilla married late in life, and witnessed the wedding of sister Alfretta in 1888 who was the only one to have offspring: Vera Muriel Irwin (1893-1943) who married Edward Honan, and 'Mac' Irwin (1901-1980).

PAGE TWO

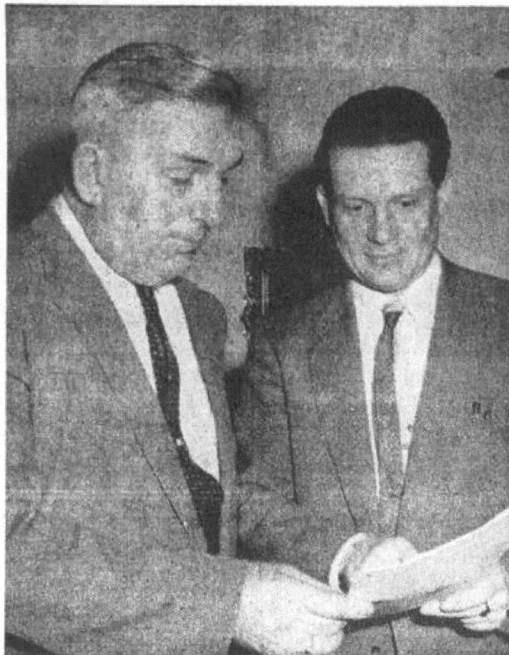

What The Tuberculin Test Is

With the Tuberculin Test and Chest X-ray in operation now in Durham County, many people will be interested in knowing just what the tuberculin test is.

It is a simple test to find out whether or not there are tuberculosis germs in the body. A harmless substance called tuberculin is injected under the skin, usually on the forearm, where it is easy to see the results—if there are any, from two to four days later the test is inspected or 'read'. In the great majority of cases, nothing happens. This means there are no TB germs in the body. As long as there are no germs, there will be no TB. Sometimes there is redness and a roughness, caused by a slight hardening into small bumps. The tecnical terms is 'induration'. This is called a positive reaction.

Ninety-nine times out of a hundred, this does not mean a person has tuberculosis. A great many persons get some TB germs into their bodies without developing TB. A person who is positive should have a chest X-ray at once. If, as is usually the case, there is no disease, the doctor should be asked for advice about a regular check-up, and how often.

Those who have a positive reaction to tuberculin, and everyone over forty, even though they are not reactors, should have periodic chest X-rays. After 40, quite a few persons develop heart and lung diseases, which are not tuberculosis or infectious, but are serious. The doctor's chances of dealing with them successfully are improved if they are found early.

Executives Plan TB Test

Mr. McNall Irwin, Chairman of districts for the Durham Tuberculin Test, and Chest X-ray, and Mr. A. E. Rafuse of Cobourg, Treasurer of the Northumberland-Durham TB Association at a recent organizational meeting.

You Can Depend On

Figure 37 McNall 'Mac' Irwin, Durham TD. Canadian Statesman (Bowmanville, ON), 18 Jun 1959, p. 2

This is the only photo I could find of Mr Mac Irwin in the Canadian Statesman. His interests were wide, from the Zion United Church to the Durham Tuberculin Test to the farmers' association and as the proprietor of the Tait properties, namely the Coronation Restaurant and the Octagon House. (I think Mr Carmen Irwin takes very closely after his father.)

tion than the cultivation of cruelty.

* * *

NEW DRESS FOR THE OCTAGON

What a pleasure to see Bowmanville's old Octagon House shining in a coat of new white stucco! We congratulate the owner, Mr. Mac Irwin, on the fine appearance of the Octagon, which as we told about a year ago, was designed by Mr. W. H. Heu de Bourck, the Congregational minister here from 1876 to 1881.

Mr. Heu de Bourck chose this unusual design for the parsonage of the Congregational Church, and it has since been one of the landmarks of the town. It must be almost 80 years old now, but in its new dress it is as bright and distinctive as a new button.

* * *

OF SHOES AND SHIPS ETC

Figure 41. Mac Irwin paints the Octagon House, 1956 July 26 Canadian Statesman

MORRISH

(Intended for last week)

We were sorry to hear of Mrs. William (Bertha) Hamilton moving to Port Hope after nearly 60 years spent in the lovely farm home one mile north of Morrish Church. Since the death of her husband William, our neighbour has lived alone. With advancing years her family were anxious that their mother move to a less lonesome location, and the last week of October her daughter Winnifred, Mrs. M. Brimacombe of Bunker Hill, and Kathleen, Mrs. Austin, Port Hope, saw their mother comfortably settled in her new home, Harcourt St., Port Hope. We extend the good wishes of this community for many happy years in her new home.

The many friends in our small village extend the deepest sympathy to Mr. and Mrs. M. Irwin and family in their recent bereavement of a loving father and grandfather, the late Mr. Bruce Crossley, a well known farmer of Roseberry Hill. The late Mr. Crossley was a quiet and retiring nature, a good neighbour and friend of many. He will be sadly missed by a large circle of relatives, friends and neighbours.

Mrs. Vera Anderson is spending a few days with friends at Millbrook.

Hallowe'en passed off very quietly in our community and the much needed rain failed to dampen the spirit of hobgoblin and fairy tale characters this ghostly evening. There were many cries of "Trick or Treat," and all visitors received a hearty welcome. A "Turkish Princess"

Figure 38. Canadian Statesman, 13 Nov 1963

Mrs Barbara Irwin, his daughter-in-law, (married to Mr Carmen Irwin) had mentioned in passing that Mr Mac Irwin may have been a farmer of Roseberry Hill but he was very active throughout the townships of Darlington and Clarke, west to Bowmanville and elsewhere on business. People certainly knew him as the owner of the Octagon House — and what he was doing with the then-80 year old property. On July 26, 1956 edition of the Canadian Statesman, page 4, in bold is a snippet "New Dress for the Octagon" - congrats Mac Irwin on new white paint on the stucco on the Octagon.

The early newspapers are physical copies of what ia present-day Facebook. Residents notified columnists about their dinner guests, travels, and who is in hospital. As some half-wit once said, Hatched, Matched. Dispatched.

Two Hope Farmers Have Narrow Escape With Runaways

A Hope Township boy Wednesday suffered severe bruises when dragged a considerable distance by a runaway horse.

Lawrence Boyko, son of Sam Boyko, Osaca, and popular Port Hope High School student, had finished raking hay and was opening a gate to leave the field when the horse bolted.

It is understood the horse kicked at a fly and somehow got his leg over the shaft frightening him into bolting. In an attempt to get on the rake, young Boyko fell in front of the fast-moving vehicle.

Results of X-rays are not known at the present time, but the rake was completely destroyed and the horse severely injured. A veterinarian disposed of the animal.

Lawrence Boyko is a very likeable lad, according to neighbors, who expressed a desire to wish him a speedy recovery.

The hissing noise produced from a tobacco spray under pressure Thursday frigtened two horses on the farm of McNall Irwin, R. R. 3, Port Hope, and they ran away.

The sprayer was completely wrecked but no other damage was done. Neither the horses nor Mr. Irwin was injured.

shore Intermediate Baseball League, local fans are only being human when they'cry for keener competition.

So far this season the Roses have chalked up 21 wins while dropping only one game. Whitby trimmed the "Brooks" 6-1 earlier in the season.

But listen closely, fans. The Roses—always eager to oblige—will answer the common cry for competition at the B.H.S. ball park on Thursday, July 31.

The boys are stepping over their heads into Senior water. They'll take on the Oshawa Merchants, Ontario Sr. Champions in 1951, and present leaders in the Niagara Baseball League. The game starts at 6 p.m.

So let it be said that the Roses are doing everything in their power to please their loyal supporters. The game should prove to be the best of the season even though it's strictly an exhibition tilt.

Port Man Wins Free Detroit Trip

The Brookdale Roses draw for an all expense trip to Detroit was Saturday evening won by W. R. Simpson of Port Hope.

Manager Maxie Yourth sold the winning ticket and he, too, comes in for a free Detroit trip. It is understood, however, that both took $100 cash instead of the trip prize.

Local Girl a Victim of Polio Rehabilitated Through the Efforts Of the Paraplegic Association

During the last few years we have been hearing more and more about rehabilitation of the physically handicapped. A rehabilitation organization of particular interest to the people of Bowmanville, in the Canadian Paraplegic Association which has been instrumental in helping Miss Jean Rundle of O'Dell St., daughter of Mrs. Sherwood Rundle.

Miss Rundle was in excellent

Miss Rundle says that this old world isn't such a bad place after all, for only when one meets with trouble does one realize fully how many kind people there are. A good example of this is Mrs. Art Hunpage and the Sunshine Club. Recently these local ladies learned Miss Rundle needed a new wheel chair, so they at once went to work and bought

Figure 40. runaway horse, Mac Irwin, Canadian Statesman, 24 Jul 1952

BOWMANVILLE, OCT. 26th, 1922.

LOCAL AND OTHERWISE

The concert and social at the Oddfellow's Hall was a great treat.

Bazaar and supper Tuesday, Nov. 7, Methodist Church at 3 and 5 p. m. Buy winter needs before prices advance. See McMurtry & Co's ad.

Miss Eva Moore, Toronto, is visiting her aunt, Mrs. E. Rutledge.

BIRTHS

FOUND—At Severance Hospital, Seoul, Korea, on Wednesday, October 20, to Dr. and Mrs. Norman Found (nee Helen Cass) a son (Norman Paul). Both doing well.

MARRIAGES

CROSSLEY—IRWIN—At Welcome, Ont., on Oct. 19th, by Rev. J. F. Mears, Hazel Lorene, only daughter of Mr. and Mrs. B. W. Crossley of Zion, to Mr. H. L. McNall Irwin, son of Mr. and Mrs. E. Irwin, Charlecote.

Figure 39. Henry Luther McNall Irwin marries Hazel Crossley 1922

Mac Irwin and his wife Hazel (Crossley) Irwin had two children, Thelma Irwin (who married Norman Earl of Ida, Ontario) and Carmen L Irwin.

BOWMANVILLE - apartment, including appliances and facilities. Available June 1st. $180 month. Easy access to 401 and Hwy. 2. Phone 983-5016 or 987-5017.   22-TFN

TWO bedroom apartment in the Octagon, heated, reasonable rent plus hydro. Adults preferred. Available July 1st. Phone 1-786-2680.   23-1N

5 ROOM apartment, 4 pc. bath, large kitchen and living room. $150 plus utilities. Maple Grove area. Phone 728-5213.   23-1N

Figure 42. Octagon apt - Jun 7, 1978 Canadian Statesman

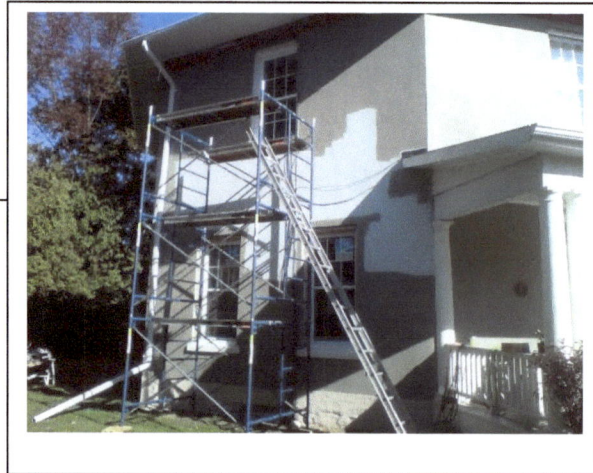

Figure 43. back from surgery Peterborough - Canadian Statesman (Bowmanville, ON), 7 Nov 1973

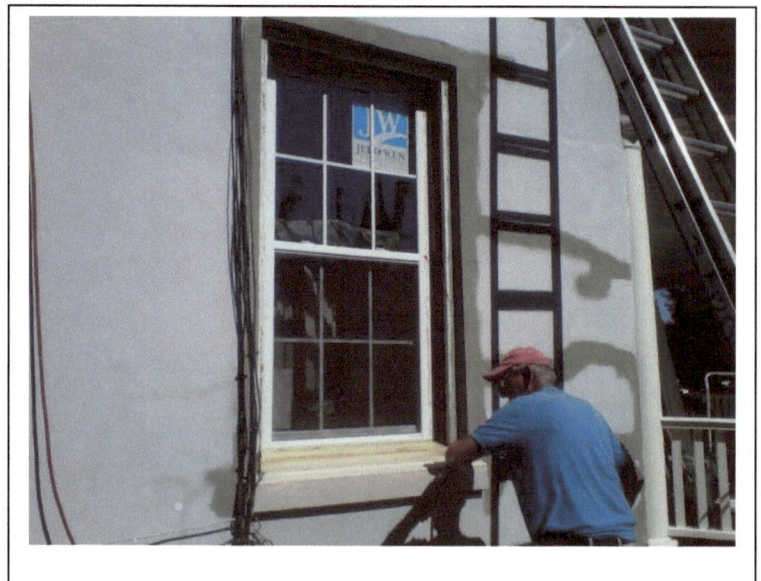

Dated at Bowmanville, this 13th day of June, 1949.

THE DOMINION ELECTIONS ACT

FINALLY REVISED URBAN LIST OF ELECTORS

Electoral District of Durham, Town of Bowmanville.
Urban Polling Division No. 54 (Bow. 5).

Comprising: Includes all that part of the said Town lying South of the centre line of Wellington Street extended parallel to King Street to the Easterly Limits East of Temperance Street and North of the centre line of Church St. extended parallel to Wellington Street.

The following names have been enumerated during a recent house-to-house visitation in the above mentioned polling division by a pair of urban enumerators:—

BROWN STREET

6 Hawes, Ruth, housewife	1
6 Reid, Delbert, railway section man	2
6 Reid, Mrs. Delbert —	3

CHURCH STREET

18 Harvey, Frank, mechanic	4
18 Harvey, Mrs. Frank —	5
32 Stutt, Ralph, manager	6
32 Stutt, Mrs. Ralph —	7
36 Wright, Thomas, rubber worker	8
36 Wright, Mrs. Thomas —	9
36 Wright, Joan, spinster	10
36 Wright, Ross, rubber worker	11
38 McCulloch, Neil, gentleman	12
38 McCulloch, Mrs. Neil	13
38 Quinn, Wm., gentleman	14
38 Quinn, Mrs. Wm. —	15
44 Fry, Ray, foreman	16
44 Fry, Mrs. Ray —	17
44 Fry, Robert, gentleman	18
44 Fry, Mrs. Robert —	19
46 McKnight, Samuel, gentleman	20
46 Miller, Theodore, mechanic	21
46 Miller, Mrs. Theodore —	22
48 Preston, David, decorator	23
48 Preston, Stanley, decorator	24
48 Preston, Mrs. Stanley —	25
50 Dale, Arthur, H., sectionman	26
50 Reid, Bernard, gentleman	27
50 Wakelin, Rosalind, widow	28
54 Worden, Mrs. Ethel —	29
56 Cole, Wm., rubber worker	30
56 Cole, Mary, Jane, widow	31
60 Thompson, Francis, rubber worker	32
60 Thompson, Mrs. Francis —	33
64 Purdy, Mrs. G. Fred	34
64 Purdy, G. Fred, rubberworker	35
64 Thompson, Earl, Gen. Motors worker	36
64 Thompson, Mrs. Earl —	37
68 Murphy, Hugh, rubber worker	38
68 Murphy, Mrs. Hugh —	39
70 Mavin, Albert, rubber worker	40
70 Mavin, Mrs. Albert —	41
74 Chase, George, hydro manager	42
74 Chase, Mrs. George —	43
74 Watson, Mrs. Anna, clerk	44
78 Robson, Oswald, agent	45
78 Robson, Mrs. Oswald —	46
82A Gilhooley, Mrs. Donald —	47
82A Gilhooley, Donald, —	48
82 Mogan, James, bank clerk	49
82 Tighe, Mrs. Hilda	50
82 Tighe, Miss Helen, bookkeeper	51
84 Baptiste, Mrs. Geo.	52
84 Baptiste, George, C.N.R. agent	53
84 Wight, Melbourne, nurseryman	54
84 Wight, Mrs. Melbourne —	55
86 O'Rourke, Norman, draftsman	56
86 O'Rourke, Mrs. Norman —	57
90 Densem, Mrs. Mary, widow	58
86 Short, James, clerk	59
90 Grieve, Mrs. Julia	60
90 Ormiston, W. J. E., foreman	61
90 Ormiston, Mrs. W. J. E. —	62
94 Anderson, Clifford, linesman	63
94 Anderson, Mrs. Clifford —	64
94 Comstock, Mrs. Pearl —	65
94 Haig, Miss Dorothy, teacher	66
94 Mutton, Miss Rena, teacher	67

CHURCH STREET—Cont.

98 Colville, Mrs. Alex, widow	68
98 King, Mrs. Margaret, rubber worker	69
98 Rundle, Chas., rubber worker	70
100 McFeeters, Chas., polisher	71
100 McFeeters, Mrs. Chas. —	72
100 McFeeters, George, merchant	73
100 McFeeters, Miss Violet, clerk	74
106 Slemon, Mrs. C. W. —	75
107 Slemon, C. W., doctor	76
114 Dewell, Alfred, rubber worker	77
114 Dewell, Mrs. Alfred —	78
114 Dewell, Miss Gertrude, nurse	79
116 Dilling, Forrest, A., bookkeeper	80
116 Dilling, Mrs. Forrest, A. —	81
118 Shackleton, John, laborer	82
118 Shackleton, Mrs. John —	83
240 Froats, Stanley, machinist	84
240 Froats, Mrs. Stanley —	85
242 Allen, Marvin, truck driver	86
242 Allen, Mrs. Marvin —	87
242 Atchison, LLoyd K., mechanic	88
242 Atchison, Mrs. LLoyd K., teacher	89
242 Berry, Leland, accountant	90
242 Berry, Mrs. Leland —	91
242 Gallagher, Robt., salesman	92
242 Gallagher, Mrs. Robt. —	93
242 Parker, Lionel, plumber	94
242 Parker, Mrs. Lionel —	95

DIVISION STREET

45 Mason, Mrs. Chas., widow	96
46 Austin, Dr. Chas. J., doctor	97
46 Austin, Mrs. Chas. J. —	98
48 Brooking, Howard, decorator	99
48 Brooking, Mrs. Howard, nurse	100
48 Hannan, Norman, garage service	101
48 Hannan, Mrs. Norman —	102
48 Slingerland, Wm., Motors worker	103
48 Slingerland, Mrs. Wm. —	104
49 Smith, Aubrey, funeral director	105
49 Smith, Mrs. Aubrey —	106
49 Wood, Lewis R., gentleman	107

GEORGE STREET

16 Rowe, John L., rubber worker	108
16 Rowe, Mrs. John L. —	109
20 Marlowe, Mrs. Edith, rubber worker	110
20 Cook, Frank, canners laborer	111
23 Rowe, John M., painter	112
23 Rowe, Mrs. John M. —	113
23 Rowe, Donald M., clerk	114
23 Rowe, Miss Francis, civil servant	115
24 Barton, Wm. L., farmer	116
24 Barton, Miss Olive, nurse	117
24 Brown, George, gentleman	118
25 Coffey, Rev. S. J., clergyman	119
25 O.Donoghue, Margaret, housekeeper	120

ONTARIO STREET

1 Tapson, Mrs. Emma —	121
2 Wilson, Paul, machinist	122
2 Wilson, Mrs. Paul —	123
2 Wilson, Miss Sheila, clerk	124
5 Jones, Reginald, factory manager	125
5 Jones, Mrs. Reginald —	126
6 Northcott, Arley, funeral director	127
6 Northcott, Mrs. Arley —	128

Figure 44. Statesman, 30

at convalesence.

Zion (Hope Township)

(Intended for last week)

Mr. and Mrs. Chas. Meneilley were recent overnight guests of Mr. and Mrs. John Meneilley, Belleville.

Mr. Fred Roby, Miss Hilda and Mrs. C. Meneilley spent Thursday in Stirling.

Mr. Harry Traver, Fenwick, was with his daughter and son-in-law, Mr. and Mrs. Chas. Roby for the Thanksgiving weekend.

Mr. and Mrs. Joseph Segar and family, North Bay, spent their holiday with Mrs. Segar's parents, Mr. and Mrs. Elsworth Caswell.

Mr. and Mrs. McNall Irwin were Thanksgiving dinner guests of their daughter and family, Mr. and Mrs. Norman Earl, Ida.

Mrs. Norman Gerow and David spent the holiday weekend with relatives in Wellington and Picton.

Mr. and Mrs. C. Meneilley spent several days last week with relatives in Orillia and Waubaushene.

Get Cash Today For Old Appliances

through
STATESMAN

DIVISION STREET
48 Apt. 1, Huffman, Harry, prov. police ....
48 Apt. 1, Huffman, Mildred — ....
48 Apt. 2, Kostka, Douglas, prov. police ....
48 Apt. 2, Kostka, Dorothy — ....
48 Apt. 3, Marshall, George, hydro worker ....
48 Apt. 3, Marshall, Helen R. — ....

Figure 48. 1953 Voters List

48 Apt. 1 Wheaton, Russell, bookkeeper ...
48 Apt. 1 Wheaton, Mrs. Shirley — ....
48 Apt. 2 Beers, John, G.M.C. ....
48 Apt. 2 Beers, Mrs. Patricia — ....
48 Apt. 3 Morrill, Mrs. Maud, widow ....
48 Apt. 4 Belanger, Mrs. — ....

Figure 47. 1958 Voters List

48 Apt. 1 Shaw, Miss Kathleen, spinster ....
48 Apt. 2 Honeyman, Mrs. Katherine, widow
48 Apt. 3 Morrill, Mrs. Maud, widow
48 Apt. 4 Lundy, Frank, teacher
48 Apt. 4 Lundy, Mrs. Dorothy
48 Smith, Mrs. Aubrey, widow

Figure 45. 1963 voters list

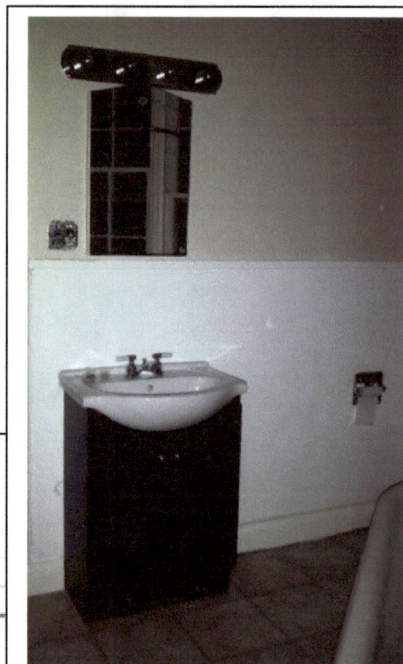

48 1 Shaw, Miss Kathleen, Spinster ....
48 2 Honeyman, Mrs. Katharine, Widow ...
48 3 Morrill, Mrs. Maud, Widow ....
48 4 Brooks, Mrs. Edith, Widow ....
48 4 Brooks, Miss Edith, Cashier ....

Figure 46. 1965 Voters List

Voters List from another year shows 4 apartments

DIVISION STREET

45 Walters, Rex, Rural Hydro _____
45 Walters, Mrs. Mary — _____
46 Austin, Charles, Doctor _____
46 Austin, Mrs. Elba — _____
46 Austin, Miss Patricia, Clerk Typist __
48 Apt. 1, Shaw, Mrs. Ethel _____
48 Apt. 2, Honeyman, Mrs. Catherine ___
48 Apt. 3, Morrill, Mrs. Maude, _____
48 Apt. 4, Brooks, Mrs. Edith _____
48 Apt. 4, Brooks, Miss Edith M., Sec. __

Figure 49. Voters List 1968 - Octagon House 4 apt (from Judy Vinish Mann)

48 Apt. 1 Cryderman, Mrs. Alba, widow...
48 Apt. 2 Biflett, Mrs. Sarah, widow.......
48 Apt. 3 Shaw, Mrs. Ethel, widow ....
48 Apt. 4 Gilmer, Mrs. Ethel, widow.......

Figure 50. Voters List 1972 (from Judy Vinish Mann)

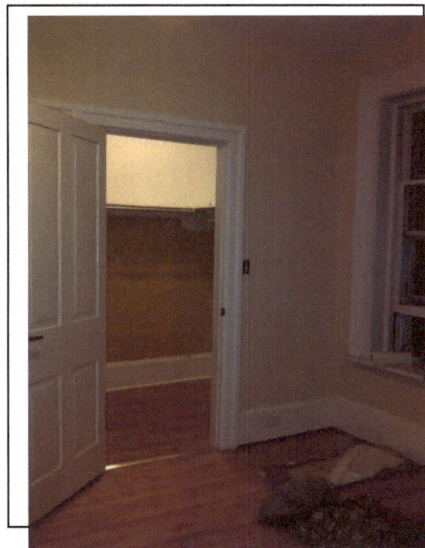

Chapter 8. 'Young' Carmen

Urge Preservation of Corner in Bowmanville

The municipality's heritage committee wants to make sure that one of Bowmanville's most historic four corners is preserved for posterity.

At a meeting Monday, Newcastle council was asked to designate the four houses at the corner of Division and Wellington Sts., for protection against the march of time.

The Local Architectural Conservation Advisory Committee (LACAC), suggested in a letter to council that establishing a heritage conservation district at the four corners would provide an example of different and characteristic architecture within the town. The four homes would be protected from demolition or changes to their facades.

Of the buildings being considered for special protection, the oldest is the Waltham Cottage on 49 Division St. which was built in 1856. The remaining homes are of a similar age and include the Prower House, the Trebilcock House and the Octagon House.

Council agreed Monday to put the wheels in motion in order to protect the buildings listed by the Heritage committee. However, elected officials were told that there is no money in the budget this year to designate the homes for special protection.

Designating buildings as historic sites means advertising the proposed designation and setting restrictions on the use of the buildings.

Councillor Maurice Prout said he wondered if the owners understood the restrictions that would be placed on their property and added that he understood they would not be able to do a thing to their houses unless they came to Council. The Bowmanville Councillor also suggested that there are some other historic buildings outside of Bowmanville which also should be considered for special protection.

Referring to council's approval of the request from LACAC, Mayor Rickard said "this puts the wheels in motion." He added that final conservation of the buildings for their architectural value may eventually happen or it may not.

Around the time Mrs Mac Irwin (Hazel) became the proprietor of the Octagon House (after 1980 and later, her son, 'young Carmen'), residents of the town became more active in the preservation of Bowmanville's architectural history.

THURSDAY, MAY 1st, 1952

week in observation and practice at the local school. While in the district they stayed with Mrs. C. Raby.

Messrs. Harold, Brian and Ellsworth Caswell motored to Apsley and district on Sunday.

Mrs. H. Caswell and Iris attended a showing of Mexican pictures by Mr. A. Holmes, Toronto.

Mr. Roger Tamblyn is spending several days in Port Hope Hospital for observation.

Congratulations and best wishes to Mr. and Mrs. Carmen Irwin who were married on April 19 in St. Paul's Church, Perrytown. Mrs. Irwin is the former Miss Barbara Wilson, daughter of Mr. and Mrs. J. Edwin Wilson, Garden Hill.

Mr. and Mrs. Traver, Fenwick, visited their daughter and son-in-law, Mr. and Mrs. C. Raby.

East of the school the pupils had the beautiful sight of a doe and fawn standing in the clearing, then rising gracefully over a fence as a collie startled them with sudden staccato barks.

HER'S DAY

Figure 51. Barbara Wilson marries Carmen Irwin - Canadian Statesman (Bowmanville, ON), 1 May 1952

Historic designation
Four corners of Wellington and Division Streets:

South-west – The **Octagon House** (1864) 48 Division
North-west - **Prower House** – (1858) 86 Wellington
North-east – **Trebilcock House/John McClung** – (Northcutt Elliot)
South-east – **Waltham Cottage** (1856) 49 Division

WESLEYVILLE

Hope township charge of the United Church held its worship service on the lawns of the Carmen Irwin home on Sunday morning, July 16th. Chairs were placed under the spreading branches of huge Norway maple and catalpa trees for the sun was bright and hot. The view of flower gardens and landscaped ponds with Canada geese and a family of baby ducks, made a beautiful and restful setting for worship. It was conducted by Rev. F. Linstead, Morley Bickle was organist and the choir members were all ladies. They sang, "Have thine own way Lord" and another number during the offering. Rev. Linstead used readings to tell of the difficulty of presenting Jewish law to new Gentile Christian converts and clarification of the law from the Sermon on the Mount. His message to the children told of the difference in freedom of worship from the times Christians had to meet in secret in the catacombs of home and today's privilege of worshipping where we please. "Unto the hills around" was his text for a review of great events of the church occurring on hills. Beginning with Sinai called the hill of law, the sermon on the mount and Calgary. Finally there is the hill of Hope. Jewish people still look for the coming of the Messiah while Christian pray for "Thy Kingdom come". God has given us the gospel of love and for all mankind there is God's grace.

The offering was received by John Irwin, Bill Bickle, Allin Osborne and Robert Symons. Following the service, the congregation remained for coffee. Next Sunday's service will be at the home of Mr. and Mrs. Reg McCool, Canton.

There was a happy gathering at Welcome Sunday School room last Wednesday evening, July 12th when about 70 friends from the surrounding communities came to shower Marie Irwin with gifts and good wishes. The room was decorated with pink and white streamers, bells and balloons. Two tables also covered in pink and white, were piled high with parcels

and guests spent the minutes before Marie's arrival, in a contest to name household articles using the letters of her name. Marie was escorted to the tables blindfolded as she had been brought from home, so the first things the saw when she was unmasked were the laden tables and rows of smiling faces. A corsage of everlasting flowers was pinned on her dress by Mrs. L. Boyko. Margaret Harness and Jennifer Lord assisted her in opening the parcels, which revealed almost every accessory needed in her kitchen, dining room and towels and bed coverings as well. Jane Boyko helped pass the gifts to rows of guests for viewing. As she finished, one of her assistants punctured the balloon over her head, releasing a shower of confetti. Marie thanked her friends and invited them to visit her in her and her future husband's home in Warkworth. Their marriage takes place in the near future.

Congratulations to local young people, Edward Henderson, Andrew McColl and Aileen Wilson who, with others from Port Hope High School, were named Ontario Scholars as they graduated.

Mr. and Mrs. Ken Dinner and Mr. and Mrs. Archie Ford returned on Saturday from a month's tour of the Canadian west.

Bill Barrowclough and family of Peterborough and Mr. and Mrs. Arthur Martin of Kingston visited with Harold Barrowclough on Sunday.

Representatives of Eldorado have been holding meetings in the area to answer questions and explain why they are studying different sites for a new plant. A small number of people are invited to attend by the host. One meeting was held at Truman Austin's on Monday evening and by the nature of the small group there was little argument. Some are in favour

Figure 52. Irwin farm hosts summer church services, July 19, 1978

Around this time, I recall slipping out the back of the Coronation Restaurant and encountering some well-dressed official types from Town Hall in the laneway remarking on the old warehouse building. They nodded to me, saying they were doing their rounds and I thought nothing more of it apart from mentioning it to Dad. Then the next edition of the Canadian Statesman came out with photos of town councilors pointing out safety issues having to do with the building! Who says there is no bad publicity? My sisters and I were on the brink of marching over to Town Hall when Dad picked up the phone to the Irwins. To this day, I have no idea what Mr Irwin did, but suffice it to say, the Keystone Kops never trespassed on his property ever again.

.

NEWTONVILLE

Mr. and Mrs. Frank Ovens and Barbara returned from their Western trip last Tuesday.

Mrs. Jeffry of Toronto spent a few days with her sister, Mrs. Fred Saunders, recently.

Millbrook Girls played Newtonville team, here, last Monday night, the locals winning 10-5.

Misses Diane and Irene Kimball both underwent tonsil operations in Memorial Hospital last week.

Mrs. Bruce Elliott with Mr. and Mrs. Russell Elliott and family, Oshawa, enjoyed a motor trip to Portland, Maine, lately.

Over forty ladies and three gentlemen embarked on the bus trip last Wednesday, sponsored by Newtonville Women's Institute. Leaving here at 9 a.m. they drove to Toronto where the bus parked, and all boarded the schooner "Sam McBride" for the trip across the lake to Centre Island. After dinner and some brief sight-seeing, the return trip to Toronto and the waiting bus was made, and the tourists headed for Pioneer Village where the thermometer registered about 85° in the shade! However, the various places of interest were all visited and enjoyed, ending with the Museum, to which place we were conveyed by team of horses, hitched to the Conestoga wagon. Once more we boarded the bus and headed home to Newtonville. Those going from here included Mrs. S. Lancaster, Mrs. M. Jones, Mrs. A. Wade, Mrs.

Watt. Mrs. M. Samis, Mrs. W. Prouse, Mrs. M. Irwin, Mrs. W. Milligan, Mrs. C. Brown, Mrs. T. Henderson, Mrs. H. Burley, Mrs. B. Skelding, Miss B. Milligan, Mrs. R. Farrow, Ken and friend, Mr. Grant Wade, Mrs. J. Elliott and Dorothy, Mrs. Boisvert and daughter, Miss Joan Walkey, Mrs. W. Wood, Mrs. Oudshoorn, Mrs. H. Trim, Mrs. S. Hallowell, Mrs. G. Trim, Mrs. G. McCullough and Mrs. F. Gilmer.

Local Girls entertained the Newcastle team on Wednesday night and lost by the score of 15-9.

Visitors with Mr. Raymond Bruce last weekend included Mr. and Mrs. W. Jinkens, Bancroft, and Mrs. Marjorie Dafoe of Millbridge.

Mr. Bruce Elliott Jr. spent last week with Mr. Bain Parfitt at Washago.

Mr. and Mrs. Harry Wade have been holidaying the past two weeks in Flin Flon, Manitoba.

Mr. and Mrs. Joe Dubeau and family have been away on a camping trip at Bon Echo.

Master Barry Lane has been visiting Mr. and Mrs. Charles Gray, in Bowmanville.

Mrs. F. Nesbitt was a recent visitor with Mr. and Mrs. Wellington Farrow, Newcastle.

Janetville Men's Softball team played here last Tuesday night, losing to Newtonville by the score of 16-5.

Mr. and Mrs. Jack Moore of Hamilton, with Mr. and Mrs. Chester Hill of Buffalo, spent a few days last week with Mr. and Mrs. C. H. Lane at their cottage.

Mr. Raymond Trim, with Mr. Bert Trim and Mr. Bill Fox, is away on a fishing trip.

Mr. and Mrs. Phil Gilmer

ALEK TRICIAN SAYS
THE STORY HAS REALLY GOTTEN

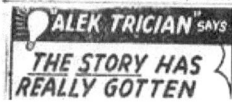

Figure 53. United Church Women bus trip to Toronto, Statesman. July 31, 1963

The Irwins hosted summer church services at their farm as well as the not-to-be-missed annual BBQ. Mrs Barbara Irwin is a keen gardener as well, member in Bowmanville and Port Hope horticultural societies.

Whenever the Irwins dropped by the restaurant for supper or lunch or coffee, Dad was always glad to see them. He made a huge fuss over old Mrs Irwin (Hazel), which was out of genuine respect, not just paying homage to the landlady.

Once a year Dad would drive us girls with him down around Christmas to her home east of Newtonville (over the years, the Irwin listing in the phone book bounced from Newtonville to Welcome to Port Hope, although Mrs Irwin always lived in the same darling house on the south side of Highway 2.) Always the same patter, an interval of 'older people talking', we knew what followed was a pot of tea, a plate of cookies and often a freshly-baked cake, quite a treat as Dad and Mom did not allow us to take in too many sweets. (Dental bills were

THURSDAY, NOV. 17th, 1955

TYRONE

W.M.S. Meeting

The November meeting of the Woman's Missionary Society was held at the home of Mrs. A. Hamilton with 18 ladies and three children present. Pres. Mrs. J. C. Cook presided.

It was decided to sell hotdogs, doughnuts and coffee at the sale of the late Mr. Wallace Miller on Saturday.

Miss Grace Smith, group leader, and Miss Jean Philp gave the worship period; a reading by Mrs. S. T. Hoar, piano solo by Mrs. F. Jackson and Mrs. Ralph Glaspell presented the chapter of the study book which was very interesting. Dainty lunch was served.

Mission Band

Mission Band was held Sunday morning with an attendance of 15. Vice-President Patsy Gibbs presided and Carrol McRoberts as secretary. President Lauraine Cook gave the devotional. Kenneth Murphy received the offering. Mrs. Rahm told a story from the study book.

Mr. and Mrs. J. Gibbs and Michael visited at Mr. and Mrs. R. Perfects and Mr. and Mrs. G. Perfects, Bowmanville.

Mrs. W. Miller and Douglas visited Mr. and Mrs. Clinton English, Bridgenorth.

Messrs. George Hynes, Willowdale, and Robert Hynes, Stouffville, visited their brother, John Hynes.

Diane Slobodian spent the weekend with Mr. and Mrs. John Mitruk, Oshawa.

Mr. and Mrs. James Park and children, Peterborough, visited Mr. and Mrs. Walter Park Jr.

Mr. and Mrs. Howard Brent were dinner guests on Sunday of Mrs. R. J. Cassidy, Toronto.

Mr. and Mrs. George Willis,

Ray and Vernon, Cannington; Mr. and Mrs. J. Murdoh and boys, Bowmanville, with Mr. and Mrs. F. L. Byam.

Mr. and Mrs. F. L. Byam visited her sister, Mrs. L. Robinson who is in the Port Hope Hospital and is very ill.

Mr. and Mrs. T. Findlay, Mr. and Mrs. Gordon Walker and children, Unionville, with Mrs. Otto Virtue.

Mr. and Mrs. A. Youngman and boys visited Mr. and Mrs. Ed. Youngman, Pontypool.

Congratulations to Mrs. Arthur Brent who celebrated her birthday on Saturday. Mr. and Mrs. Ross Pooley, Oshawa, entertained the Brent family on Saturday night to a turkey dinner at the home of Mr. and Mrs. A. H. Brent.

ZION (Hope Township)

Mr. McNall Irvun and son, Carmen, Have joined forces in the north country in search of the fleet-foot.

Mr. Harry Morrison, Washago, was a guest at the Meneilley home, Saturday.

Mrs. Harold Caswell is spending this weekend with her daughter, Mrs. Robert Brice, Port Hope, while Mr. Brice is deer-hunting.

The regular meeting of the W.A. will be held at the church Thursday afternoon, Nov. 17. Roll call, a donation to "wishing well" for the bazaar, Nov. 25.

Mrs. Carmen Irwin and daughter are visiting her parents, Mr. and Mrs. Wilson, Garden Hill.

Play practice was held at Mrs. Meneilley's Monday night. This will be given Nov. 25, following the bazaar.

something our parents could not budget too much for.) After that, we were excused to explore the piano and the furniture in the formal living room. Looking back, this room was full of pieces from Archie Tait's store and Mrs Tait's Octagon House.

Occasionally, we would visit during the summer – with permission, we tried to the ring the bell on top of the garage and pump the water from the well. Once we visited the farm for an entire afternoon – Marie, Ann, young Ed and John showed us their lake. The boys dared us to walk the barn beams... we were 'city folk' to them.

OPINION LETTERS

Stumping suggestion

Wednesday, April 28, 2010 6:10:00 EDT AM

Re: wasting taxpayers' money in Port Hope's Ward 2

Observations based on over 60 years of experience as a farmer and taxpayer in Ward 2, formerly Hope Township, suggest Christmas has come early for some of the help in Ward 2. Someone in the Ivory Tower at the Town Hall has rented them some useless equipment to play with. They have been observed using said equipment to rip and tear at trees and stumps along Roseberry Road. A lot of time and effort ha been exerted, resulting in a mess and very little useful results. The crew can't be blamed. They are doing what they have been ordered to c The problem seems to originate with their supervision from "head office."

As a taxpayer, I hate to see the waste of effort and money. They are using a "stumping machine" mounted on a rented Bobcat tractor with caterpillar tracks, which consists of approximately a 15- inch circular saw blade

designed to swivel about to cut trees and stumps. It tends to get tangled up with rocks and wire from fences along the roadside, and the Bobcat has constantly to be manoeuvred back and forth, sideways, up banks and down, to get into position. In a week, the crew has made very little progress along the road.

As a farmer, I've moved a lot of fence bottoms in my day. In my opinion, the best way to do the job would be to take the serviceable wood o of the road for sawmill or woodstove use. Then, come in with a backhoe and a couple of dump trucks to remove the small stumps and brus along with the rocks. In the process, the sides of the road could be ditched, improving the drainage. The debris and excess material could removed and dumped. The roadside could then be graded, sown with grass if need be, and made clear for a mower to maintain the roadsides when the job is completed. The municipality already owns the necessary equipment, eliminating the need to rent a wasteful machine.

The work could be done very quickly, at less overall expense, and the taxpayer would know that the necessary maintenance could be completed in future at low cost.

Just an aside... the question is raised. Has amalgamation of the former Township of Hope into the Municipality of Port Hope been a good idea? I don't think so. We don't need a two-tier bureaucracy.

The road workers have to take direction through a supervisor from the head office in Port Hope which in most cases does not seem to understand the problems of rural road maintenance. We should return to Hope Township, where the road crew could work directly with the property owners to accomplish the jobs when and as needed. That's my opinion!

Carmen L. Irwin RR3 Port Hope

Remembering a great lady

DAVID WILSON
Tuesday, September 9, 2008 9:00:00 EDT AM

Ida Antonia Wilson, (nee Jackson) June 16, 1902 -September 9, 2007

At the turn of the last century, Thomas and Jenny (nee Totten) Jackson left behind friends and family in Belfast, Ireland, to purse a better life in the Dominion of Canada. Canada was experiencing rapid growth and Sir Wilfrid Laurier (Canada's seventh prime minister) was encouraging immigration to fill labour shortages in the manufacturing sector.

Toronto, Canada's second largest city (behind Montreal) was expanding with a major port and railway. Streetcars and horses bustled through the streets of Toronto, as cars were still very uncommon and an extreme luxury. The city was also moving from gas lighting to electricity and Thomas, trained as an engineer in Ireland, found work as an electrician.

The Jackson family settled in the Parkdale region of Toronto, on Sorauren Avenue, where they raised four daughters, Ida, Helen, Dorothy and Margaret. The girls enjoyed school and music lessons, with Ida going on to become an accomplished pianist and violinist. The country still had a colonial mentality and the Jackson girls grew up singing God Save the King at school for the ruling monarch King George V. The family lived close to Lake Ontario, an ideal location for taking in summertime concerts and enjoying the beaches and baths of Sunnyside Park and the Lakeshore during its heyday.

Ida grew up in progressive and turbulent times. As a young teenager, the rumblings of the First World War (1914-1918) were beginning in Europe, while in Canada women were struggling to earn the right to vote (1918). During the First World War, women took over a majority o the jobs in Canada while the men were overseas fighting. Ida was part of this first generation of women to vote, work outside the home anc earn a wage. She started working as a bank teller and then took the first dietician course at the Toronto Central Technical School. She spe several summers working as a dietician at the then-renowned Bon Echo Lodge, now a Provincial Park near Kaladar, Ontario.

Although Ida was small in stature and soft-spoken, she always had a twinkle in her eye and a purpose in her step that hinted she was a for to be reckoned with. Ida's musical connections provided her an opportunity to be introduced to Edwin Wilson, a dashing young farmer from Garden Hill. On their first date, they went by horse and buggy to a strawberry social at Carmel Corners, south of Millbrook. They soon became engaged and Edwin started fixing up the house for the arrival of his future wife. Thinking that it would be quite a transition for Ida moving from the big city of Toronto to the small village of Garden Hill, Edwin installed in the farm house one of the first indoor toilets in Hop Township.

They married on October 5, 1926, and Ida quickly settled in and mastered the hard, honest work of farming. She loved the rolling hills and cool lakes of the Port Hope region. Her sisters and parents would often visit in the summer, escaping the city heat to enjoy the fresh air anc tranquillity of the Wilson farm.

Edwin and Ida were blessed with four beautiful children, Jackson, Barbara (Irwin), David and Gordon. These were difficult times to raise a family and run a farm with the Great Depression (1929-1939), followed by the Second World War (1940-45). Hired help for the farm was difficult to find as most men were fighting overseas. The Wilson children were too young to be called up to fight, and began working with th father at very early ages.

At the time, Royal Air Force (RAF) troops from England were training nearby in Trenton. During Christmas and summer leaves, the RAF me would work on the Wilson farm in exchange for a place to stay, homecooked meals and a family to be with during the holidays. Although th farm was a break for the men, their help was most welcome to the Wilson family. To Ida's delight, one year a young military cook took over her kitchen and made the entire Christmas dinner.

Ida's early training as a dietician, and the skills to make ends meet, meant her children never suffered during WWII. The Wilsons were fairly self-sufficient with a large garden, an orchard and the livestock of the farm. In later years, her grandchildren often teased Ida about her "thriftiness," but that was a necessary survival skill for her generation, a generation that could teach us all the essentials of "reduce, reuse

Chapter 9. Irwin/Seto: Coronation to Octagon

Years later, Johnny Seto family purchased 9 King Street West from the Irwins. This property was later sold it along with the Coronation Restaurant business – the location remains a Chinese restaurant, Wah Leung Garden.

When Dad passed in February 2015, Mr and Mrs Irwin drove through one of the snowiest days of the year to pay their respects. For over 60 years, it was mutual.

And it continues to the next generation.

###

Figure 54. Front door with transom and pillars, 2013

Figure 55. Front door with transom and pillars, 2014 summer

THE CORPORATION OF THE TOWN OF NEWCASTLE

BY-LAW 81-42

being a by-law to designate property at 53 Division Street, Bowmanville and 48 Division Street, Bowmanville of architectural and historical value.

WHEREAS the Ontario Heritage Act, 1974, authorizes the Council of a Municipality to enact by-laws to designate real property, including all the buildings and structures thereon to be of historic or architectural value or interest; and

WHEREAS the Council of the Town of Newcastle has caused to be served upon the owners of the lands and premises known as 53 Division Street and 48 Division Street in the former Town of Bowmanville, now in the Town of Newcastle in the Region of Durham, and upon the Ontario Heritage Foundation, notice of intention to so designate the aforesaid real property and has caused such notice of intention to be published in a newspaper having a general circulation in the municipality once for each of three consecutive weeks; and

WHEREAS the properties of 53 Division Street and 48 Division Street in the former Town of Bowmanville have a very significant historical and architectural value and interest to the Town of Newcastle and its people in that for architectural and historical reasons they form part of an important grouping of mid nineteenth century houses at the intersection of Division and Wellington Streets; and

WHEREAS the Local Architectural Conservation Advisory Committee of the Town of Newcastle has recommended that the above mentioned properties be "designated properties" under the terms of the Ontario Heritage Act; and

WHEREAS no notice of objection to the proposed designation has been served upon the Clerk of the Municipality;

NOW THEREFORE the Council of the Corporation of the Town of Newcastle ENACTS AS FOLLOWS:

1) There is designated as being of historic and architectural value of interest the real property more particularly described in Schedule "A" hereto, known as 53 Division Street and 48 Division Street in the former Town of Bowmanville, now the Town of Newcastle.

2) The Town Solicitor is hereby authorized to cause a copy of this by-law to be registered against the properties described in Schedule "A" hereto in the proper Land Registry Office.

3) The Town Clerk is hereby authorized to cause a copy of this by-law to be served upon the owners of the aforesaid properties and upon the Ontario Heritage Foundation and to cause notice of this by-law to be published in a newspaper having general circulation in the Town of Newcastle.

By-Law read a first and second time this 6th day of April 1981.

By-Law read a third and final time this 6th day of April 1981.

Garnet B Rickard
Mayor

Joseph M. McIlroy
Clerk

File No. 60.17/01.

The Royal Canadian Legion
109 King St E

Older Adults Centre
26 Beech Ave

Valley's 2000
Fish Ladder
35 Roenigk Dr

Masonic Lodge
19 King St E

Foundry
172 Wellington St

Beech Ave Walking Tour
26 Beech Ave

McClung - Kuipers House
53 Division St

West Beach and Cottages
42 West Beach Rd

The Octagon House
48 Division St

Central Public School
120 Wellington St

Ravenscraig
8 Beech Ave

KING ST W
CONCESSION ST W
REGIONAL RD 57
QUEEN ST
KING ST E
LIBERTY ST
BASELINE RD
HIGHWAY 401
HIGHWAY 401
LAKE RD
HAINES ST
WEST BEACH RD
BOWMANVILLE

Waltham Cottage
49 Division St

Crematorium
1200 Haines St

West Side Marches
180 Westbeach Rd

Veterinary Clinic
2826 Highway 2

St. Mary's Cement
400 Waverley Rd

DOORS OPEN CLARINGTON ON JUNE 14, 2014
doorsopenclarington.wordpress.com

Over 1200 people came through the Octagon at the 2014 Doors Open in Bowmanville and were able to see three rooms inside.

The Octagon House remains a private residence.

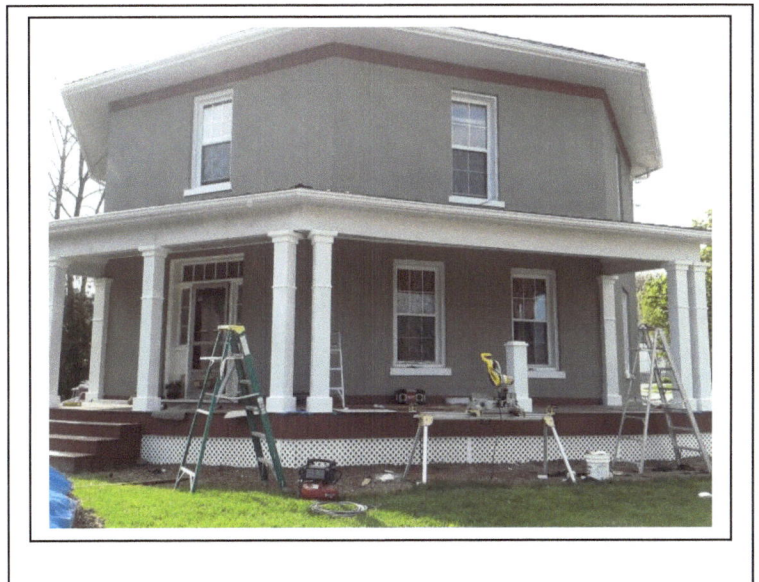

CANADA POST / POSTES CANADA *TO OVER 32,000 HOMES AND BUSINESSES IN CLARINGTON* June 2014

The beautiful Waltham Cottage was built in 1852 by Bowmanville's first mayor James McFeeters is on the Doors Open Clarington tour June 14.

Opening Doors in Bowmanville

by Bernice Norton and Charles Taws

CLARINGTON MUSEUMS
AND ARCHIVES
www.claringtonmuseums.com

Doors Open Clarington is coming again! It's the fifth year in a row and once again people are invited to take a behind-the-scenes peak at some of Clarington's most beautiful and historic places.

Every year we pick an area to explore. In the last five years our Doors Open Clarington arranged for public tours of historical buildings of Orono, Kendal, Newcastle, Newtonville and Courtice along with a number of our smaller villages and rural hidden gems.

Last year we were in Enniskillen, Haydon and Ty-

rone, and this year 2014 will see us revisit Bowmanville where we have 16 amazing sites for you to choose from. Fourteen of which have never been part of the Doors Open Clarington before!

There is something for everyone from history buffs to admirers of fine old homes to nature lovers. It's all happening on June 14th 2014 from 10:00am to 4:00pm. These 16 sites are spread out throughout the Town of Bowmanville and along the lakeshore. The Doors Open tour is a free event and you can visit as many as you like, and in any order you choose.

If fine old homes are your passion you'll have lots to see this year. The corner of Wellington and Division Streets will have three homes open for touring.

One is the unusual Octagon house. This rare eight sided house was originally built around 1864 as the manse for Trinity Congregational Church (this church building is now the Bibles for Missions Store).

Later on this house became the Tait family home of the famed Bowmanville photographer Henry C. Tait. It was also owned by his brother Archie Tait, former Bowmanville Mayor and local merchant. Some Tait family descendants will be on hand to answer questions.

The beautiful Waltham Cottage across the street will also be open. It was built in 1852 by Bowmanville's first mayor James McFeeters. This stunning example of what is now referred to as architecturally as an Ontario Cottage was later purchased

by Dr. George Humphrey Lowe for his two nieces, Catherine and Julia Welch.

These sisters ran a finishing school for young gentlewomen from the premises. This house includes many original architectural features. Be sure to take a look at the garage in the back. It was built in the 1920's and is believed to be one of the first built specifically for an automobile.

The John McClung House is known to most of you as the Northcutt-Elliott Funeral Home. This house, lovingly maintained by the present owners, is on the Doors Open tour this year (not the funeral home).

It was built in 1858 by successful merchant John McClung Sr. At one time, it looked much like the

Continued on Page 4

Figure 56 Clarington Promoter, June 2014

Selected References

Adams, Sam and Lois Adams et al. *Picture the Way We Were: A Pictorial Nostalgic Journey Through Darlington & Clarke Townships,* 1980.

Downie, Jill. *A Passionate Pen: the Life and Times of Faith Fenton,* 1996.

Garfield, Shaw et al., *Picture the Way We Were,* Bowmanville: Mothersill, 1980.

Grandfield, Diana. *Bowmanville: An Architectural and Social History (1794-1999).*

Martin, John H. *Saints. Sinners and Reformers: The Burned-Over District Re-Visited,* 2005. http://www.crookedlakereview.com/books/saints_sinners/martin12.html

Mar

Puerzer, Ellen L. *The Octagon House Inventory,* Eight-Square Publishing, 2011. http://www.octagon.bobanna.com/main_page.html

Kline, Robert, webmaster of The Octagon House Inventory http://www.octagon.bobanna.com/main_page.html

Taws, Charles D. *Bowmanville Then and Now.* Clarington: Bowmanville Museum Board, 1998.

Figure 57. Irwin men - four generations - Mac, John, Ebenezer, Carmen c 1960

Selected End Notes

[i] Lateran Bapistery, Rome. www.sacred-destinations.com/italy/rome-lateran-bapistery).

[ii] John T. Martin. Orson Fowler & Octagon,
http://www.crookedlakereview.com/books/saints_sinners/martin12.html

[iii] Kansas: A Vegetarian Utopia. https://www.kshs.org/p/kansas-historical-quarterly-kansas-a-vegetarian-utopia/13219

[iv] Frances Ingraham Heins. Octagons put edge in houses
Renewed interest in style based upon utopian ideals. New York Times News Service, March 11, 2005

[v] Octagon House, South Salem , NY USA https://www.youtube.com/watch?v=uZJZWeGa55k and
http://www.absoluteremodeling.com/Transformations.html and
http://www.westchestermagazine.com/Westchester-Magazine/Westchester-Home/Summer-2008/Sustainable-In-South-Salem/

[vi] Allen Dusault, 2007.
http://www.igreenbuild.com/_coreModules/content/contentDisplay_print.aspx?contentID=3125

[vii] Humber, William. *Bowmanville: Small Town at the Edge*. Dundurn Press, 1997.

[viii] The Congregational Magazine for the Year 1840 (formerly the London Christian Instructor) Vol 4. P 501-2
https://play.google.com/store/books/details?id=lA4EAAAAQAAJ&rdid=book-lA4EAAAAQAAJ&rdot=1

[ix] Fairbairn, J. B. *History and Reminiscences of Bowmanville*, Part 11.1906.

[x] Rev Warriner mentioned 1888
https://archive.org/stream/canadiancongrega1888cong/canadiancongrega1888cong_djvu.txt

[xi] 'Bowmanville's Congregational Church'. Montreal Daily Witness Dec 7, 1891, page 3.

[xii] Canadian Statesman (Bowmanville, ON), 28 Nov 1894, Supplement, p. 10

[xiii] Mrs Reikie gave music lessons, Canadian Statesman, 21 Aug 1907, p. 5

[xiv] Lindsay Burns nominated for her role as Faith Fenton. http://thirdstreet.ca/genevieve-pare-nominated-2014-calgary-critics-award-late-cowboy-song/

[xv] Grave of Alice Freeman 'Faith Fenton' at Mount Pleasant Cemetery, Toronto, from scottsheat
http://www.findagrave.com/cgi-bin/fg.cgi?page=gr&GRid=116018613

ABOUT THE AUTHOR

Janice Seto graduated from Bowmanville High School, holds a Bachelor of Science degree from

Victoria College, University of Toronto and completed teacher certification at Bishop's University, Quebec. Besides teaching stints in Canada, the Arctic and overseas, she studied business at the University of Victoria, and later, defended the dissertation for her doctorate in organizational psychology on the Enneagram personality system at the Professional School of Psychology in Sacramento.

With a background in sales, marketing, hospitality, labour relations, and consulting in human performance, she writes on a variety of issues and is a member of the American Psychological Association's Community College division, the Yoga Alliance and the International Enneagram Association.

Her latest books include *Johnny Seto's Bowmanville*, the sequel to *Johnny's Place: The Coronation Restaurant, Segovia Restaurant in Toronto, Get Yourself a Classroom,* a series analyzing the Betty Neels stories, JKC's Quick Guide tourism series, and has begun a series on Royalty and Enneagram.

Inquiries should be addressed to Janice(dot)seto(at)me.com

Janice Seto's homepage http://www.janiceseto.com and http://janiceseto.wix.com/words

Other books by Janice Seto also available in print and on Kindle app via Amazon.com at http://amazon.com/author/janiceseto and http://www.amazon.com/Janice-Seto/e/B00K8PN1YO